S0-BQE-581

Mentoring-Transcript Systems for Promoting Student Growth

Robert D. Brown, David A. DeCoster, *Editors*

NEW DIRECTIONS FOR STUDENT SERVICES

URSULA DELWORTH and GARY HANSON, *Editors-in-Chief*

Number 19, September 1982

Paperback sourcebooks in
The Jossey-Bass Higher Education Series

LB
2343.4
.M 45x
n.19
1982
WEST

•A15046 164671

Jossey-Bass Inc., Publishers
San Francisco • Washington • London

Mentoring-Transcript Systems for Promoting Student Growth
Number 19, September 1982
　　　Robert D. Brown, David A. DeCoster, *Editors*

New Directions for Student Services Series
Ursula Delworth and Gary R. Hanson, *Editors-in-Chief*

Copyright © 1982 by Jossey-Bass Inc., Publishers
　　　　　　　　and
　　　　　　　　Jossey-Bass Limited

Copyright under International, Pan American, and Universal
Copyright Conventions. All rights reserved. No part of
this issue may be reproduced in any form — except for brief
quotation (not to exceed 500 words) in a review or professional
work — without permission in writing from the publishers.

New Directions for Student Services (publication number USPS
449-070) is published quarterly by Jossey-Bass Inc., Publishers.
Second-class postage rates paid at San Francisco, California,
and at additional mailing offices.

Correspondence:
Subscriptions, single-issue orders, change of address notices,
undelivered copies, and other correspondence should be sent to
New Directions Subscriptions, Jossey-Bass Inc., Publishers,
433 California Street, San Francisco, California 94104.

Editorial correspondence should be sent to the Editors-in-Chief,
Ursula Delworth, University Counseling Service, Iowa
Memorial Union, University of Iowa, Iowa City, Iowa 52242
or Gary R. Hanson, Office of the Dean of Students,
Student Services Building, Room 101, University of Texas
at Austin, Austin, Texas 78712.

Library of Congress Catalogue Card Number LC 81-48581
International Standard Serial Number ISSN 0164-7970
International Standard Book Number ISBN 87589-921-8

Cover art by Willi Baum
Manufactured in the United States of America

Ordering Information

The paperback sourcebooks listed below are published quarterly and can be ordered either by subscription or as single copies.

Subscriptions cost $35.00 per year for institutions, agencies, and libraries. Individuals can subscribe at the special rate of $21.00 per year *if payment is by personal check.* (Note that the full rate of $35.00 applies if payment is by institutional check, even if the subscription is designated for an individual.) Standing orders are accepted.

Single copies are available at $7.95 when payment accompanies order, and *all single-copy orders under $25.00 must include payment.* (California, Washington, D.C., New Jersey, and New York residents please include appropriate sales tax.) For billed orders, cost per copy is $7.95 plus postage and handling. (Prices subject to change without notice.)

To ensure correct and prompt delivery, all orders must give either the *name of an individual* or an *official purchase order number.* Please submit your order as follows:

Subscriptions: specify series and subscription year.
Single Copies: specify sourcebook code and issue number (such as, SS8).

Mail orders for United States and Possessions, Latin America, Canada, Japan, Australia, and New Zealand to:
  Jossey-Bass Inc., Publishers
  433 California Street
  San Francisco, California 94104

Mail orders for all other parts of the world to:
  Jossey-Bass Limited
  28 Banner Street
  London EC1Y 8QE

New Directions for Student Services Series
Ursula Delworth and Gary R. Hanson, *Editors-in-Chief*

Contents

Editors' Notes

Thomas Patrick Melady, president of Sacred Heart University, recently warned of the growing depersonalization within institutions for post-secondary education. His plea—"Let's Not Forget the Students"—is deeply felt by an increasing number of college educators who are seeking new ways to humanize the learning process. Melady (1980) said this:

> As a university president, I sense a serious danger in higher education today. We administrators are failing to measure up to our responsibilities because in our well-meaning but time consuming efforts to achieve fiscal stability, we are losing sight of the human equation in the university experience. We are failing to spend the time to nurture meaningful relationships with students. This strikes at the very heart of our responsibilities, and I believe that this problem merits our immediate attention [p. 33].

Katz (1979) warned of similar dangers:

> Times of budgetary scarcity often go together with an undervaluation of the individual. Less caring, less service, even less courtesy, coupled with the great increase in the number of students, have increasingly made the students part of a mass. This turning of students into a passive mass of people, bereft of a sufficient sense of individuality, may become one of the most ominous effects of higher education [p. 47].

These two prominent individuals have exemplified a concern that is shared by other college educators who have witnessed the steady decline of student-centered learning over the past decade. Many experimental programs created in the 1960s and 1970s have long since been eliminated or seriously crippled through reduced funding. Perhaps even more distressing is that students describe themselves as alienated from the process of institutional decision making, recognize the powerlessness of their own student governance mechanisms, and do not perceive administrators, staff, and faculty members as caring individuals who might be personally helpful (DeCoster and Mable, 1981).

This volume of *New Directions for Student Services* provides a comprehensive review of how mentoring-transcript systems can be created and utilized to meet the developmental needs of students and humanize the college environment. The first two chapters address the major variables involved: (1) mentoring relationships between educators and students which comprise the individualized learning process, and (2) the use of student development transcripts as a means to monitor, document, and record student growth.

Chapter Three switches our attention to the national scene as Mary Kramer describes some of the variations and alternatives that have been incorporated by institutions throughout the country. Three unique programs are described in some detail by institutional representatives who serve as co-authors for this chapter: (1) The Passages Program of Azusa Pacific University (Raymond Rood). (2) The Developmental Objective/Transcript Program at the College of Saint Teresa (Martha Smith). (3) The Co-Curricular Transcript Program at the University of North Dakota (William Bryan).

In the fourth chapter, Russell Thomas, Patricia Murrell, and Arthur Chickering provide a fine commentary on the theoretical bases which underlie mentoring-transcript systems. Their discussion includes the feasibility for implementing such projects and the potential impact of mentoring-transcript systems on the learning process. In Chapter Five, Vernon Williams and Dolores Simpson-Kirkland provide the reader with a step-by-step model for the successful creation and implementation of a mentoring transcript system. Jane Baack, in Chapter Six, presents specific procedures regarding both formative and summative evaluation strategies that should be included during the planning stages of a new program. In the final chapter we synthesize and summarize the implications of mentoring-transcript systems on the future role of student affairs educators as well as upon the personal development of college students.

Robert D. Brown
David A. DeCoster
Editors

References

DeCoster, D. A., and Mable, P. *New Directions for Student Services: Understanding Today's Students,* no. 16. San Francisco: Jossey-Bass, 1981.

Katz, J. "Collaboration of Academic Faculty and Student Affairs Professionals for Student Development." In A. C. Tilley, L. T. Benezet, J. Katz, and W. Shanteau (Eds.), *The Student Affairs Dean and the President: Trends in Higher Education.* Ann Arbor, Mich.: ERIC, Counseling and Personnel Services Clearinghouse, 1979.

Melady, T. P. "Let's Not Forget the Students." *Chronicle of Higher Education,* October 14, 1980, p. 33.

Robert D. Brown is professor of education, Department of Educational Psychology and Social Foundations, University of Nebraska-Lincoln.

David A. DeCoster is dean of students and associate professor, Department of Educational Psychology and Social Foundations, University of Nebraska-Lincoln.

Mentoring relationships are powerful learning experiences that can enhance the present quality of faculty-student interactions and humanize the college environment.

Mentoring Relationships and the Educational Process

David A. DeCoster
Robert D. Brown

A father recently shared hopes for his daughter's education as she entered her freshman year of college. Not surprisingly, one of his five major concerns was that she experience a meaningful relationship with an educator who is somewhat older than herself. His hope is best described in his own words:

> *A friendship with at least one faculty member (maybe two).* Physical education or philosophy, art or accounting—I am indifferent as to the academic discipline, but I want her "turned on" by a mature mind. She needs to know the youthful thrill of worshipful adoration at the feet of a master teacher. That human feet are clay she will discover soon enough. Let her be, I pray, a late bloomer when it comes to cynicism, a zestful disciple, a Plato before a Socrates [Lassegard, 1980, p. 33].

This simple expectation—shared by parents, students, faculty, and administrators—that college provide a meaningful dialogue between students and educators is at the core of the learning process. To have a positive and lasting

R. Brown and D. DeCoster (Eds.). *New Directions for Student Services: Mentoring-Transcript Systems for Promoting Student Growth,* no. 19. San Francisco: Jossey-Bass, September 1982.

influence upon students, however, faculty contact must transcend traditional perfunctory roles of teacher and academic adviser. Relationships must be informal, continuous, caring, personal encounters which permit the exploration of a wide range of topics that interest and concern students (Wilson and others, 1975). These authors concluded that students who experience a high degree of faculty interaction

> seem to take a far more active role in their own education than do their peers. Not only are they more interested in pursuing their own intellectual interests, but they are more actively engaged in utilizing the existing resources and structures of their institutions and in changing them in directions that respond better to their needs . . . these students more often helped initiate new courses, took exams in lieu of required courses, participated in study groups among some of the students in classes, took independent study courses, served on faculty-student committees within colleges or departments, and used the available counseling service [p. 165].

With this background, then, it is not surprising that Astin (1977) reported a higher level of "student satisfaction with their college experience" was associated with faculty relationships. In straightforward terms: "Students who interact frequently with faculty are more satisfied with all aspects of the institutional experience including student friendships, variety of courses, intellectual environment, and even the administration of the institution (p. 223). Pascarella and Terenzini also found that these relationships contribute to greater academic performance and personal development (1978) as well as having a positive influence on student retention (1977). In the latter case, the authors noted that student contacts with faculty "focusing on intellectual or course related matters clearly contributed most to the discrimination between persisters and voluntary leavers" (1977, p. 550). Dicsussions with faculty members related to career planning and related concerns were a second powerful variable. Steele (1978) also identified student progress toward academic and career objectives as a factor critical to persistence in college.

Thus, the case for close, personal, and frequent one-to-one relationships between students and educators is not difficult to defend in terms of philosophical perspectives or research findings.

The remainder of this chapter examines (1) the reality of faculty-student relationships, (2) student development in postsecondary education, (3) mentoring relationships, and (4) a systematic mentoring process.

The Reality of Faculty-Student Relationships

Unfortunately, the father's dream for his college-bound daughter cited earlier may never be realized. Research on the quality and quantity of faculty-student relationships over the past two decades seems to suggest consistently that most students seldom relate to their instructors outside the classroom setting and that the only systematic mechanism for nonclassroom contacts—academic advising—is woefully inadequate. In a recent study DeCoster and Mable (1981) concluded the following:

> The most telling characteristic of meaningful faculty-student relationships is their scarcity. A general feeling among students is that the campus consists of two communication networks: A student culture and a bureaucratic structure composed of faculty and administrators. There is little expectation that members of the "system" or "establishment" will view personal relationships with students as a high priority, and in reality very few students can identify a faculty member with whom they have established a close relationship. The term "friend" is seldom, if ever, mentioned, in the context of faculty encounters [pp. 42–43].

In another study, students were asked to report their nonclassroom contacts with faculty members in six potential discussion areas during one month (Wilson and others, 1975). The percentage of students who reported no contact with faculty in each of the six areas were as follows:

1. Intellectual issues or course related matters 36%
2. Educational plans or advice 29%
3. Informal conversations or socializing 34%
4. Career plans or advice 33%
5. Campus issues or sociopolitical discourse 53%
6. Personal problems or counseling 78%

After a comprehensive review of the literature and analysis of their data, these researchers could best describe typical faculty-student relationships as infrequent and superficial. In their words: "It would appear that even in their senior year, then, most students have had only a modest amount of contact with teachers outside the classroom" (Wilson and others, 1975, p. 154). Thus, a powerful variable of the learning process is a relatively untapped resource.

Student Development in Postsecondary Education

In the study cited earlier, the researchers found "that faculty members who interacted the most frequently with their students outside the classroom held more favorable views of students generally, and they more often endorsed statements reflecting an educational philosophy that stresses faculty-student interactions and faculty concern for the whole student" (Wilson and others, 1975, p. 157). It is this fundamental premise—concern for the whole student—that is so important for a humanized educational process and yet it remains an elusive concept to transform into practice.

Almost fifteen years ago, the Committee on the Student in Higher Education (1968) reaffirmed the basic role of postsecondary education to "educate the whole person." They concluded:

> Despite our limited behavioral knowledge, the college must recognize that even its instructional goals cannot be effectively achieved unless it assumes some responsibility for facilitating the development of the total human personality. A student is not a passive digester of knowledge elegantly arranged for him by superior artists of curriculum design. He listens, reads, thinks, studies, and writes at the same time that he feels, worries, hopes, loves, and hates. He engages in all these activities not as an isolated individual but as a member of overlapping communities which greatly influence his reactions to the classroom experience. To teach the subject matter and ignore the realities of the students' life and social systems of the college is hopelessly naive [p. 6].

Subsequently a series of documents have helped define and describe total developmental concept in college. Brown (1972), for example, provided a comprehensive review of the literature and a philosophical foundation in the monograph, *Student Development in Tomorrow's Higher Education: A Return to the Academy.* He suggested that student affairs educators and their faculty counterparts need to serve in proactive roles to facilitate college student development systematically. Brown refined the role of a student development educator or mentor in more recent publications and proposed a systematic process that will be explored more fully at a later point in this chapter (1980a, 1980b, and 1980c). Parker also offered a general direction with emphasis for the developmental learning process:

> The answer may lie in the model of developmental education based on the assumption that education is a joint enterprise of the teacher and the taught, that both have a stake in the outcomes that are mutually beneficial, and that each can contribute to the planning and conduct of the learning experience [1973, p. 199].

At the University of Nebraska-Lincoln, a sample of both student affairs staff and faculty members were recently asked to rank order a list of eighteen potential outcomes of a college education (Brown and Wood, 1979). Table 1 reveals that traditional items relating to cognitive growth were ranked high by both groups of educators—critical thinking, acquisition of knowledge, communication skills, and intellectual competence. But items which relate to affective dimensions of human development were also

Table 1. Faculty and Student Affairs Rankings of Educational Outcomes
(University of Nebraska)

Outcome Item	Student Affairs Rank (N = 90)	Faculty Rank (N = 65)
Critical Thinking	1	1
Acquisition of Knowledge	2	4
Communication Skills	3	2
Intellectual Competence	4	3
Well Developed Value System	5	5
Interpersonal Skills	6	8
Personal Autonomy	7	8
Employability	7	6
Sense of Purpose	8	7
Social Consciousness	9	11
Perception of Identity	10	12
Effective Interracial Ethnic Attitude	11	15
Effective Organization of Work	12	9
Cultural Appreciation	13	12
Capability for Leisure Time Activity	14	16
Well Defined Religious Orientation	14	10
Management of Emotions	15	14
Aesthetic Appreciation	16	13

Kendall's rank order correlation coefficient of .74

Note: Modified from Brown and Wood (1979)

given high priority (for instance, well developed value system, interpersonal skills, personal autonomy, sense of purpose, social consciousness, and perception of identity). Student affairs educators and their faculty colleagues agree more regarding the priorities of a college education than might have been expected. The rank order correlation coefficient was .74 for the two groups, suggesting that the concept of "total student development" or the "education of the whole person" is recognized and valued by both faculty members and student affairs educators. A similar study conducted earlier at Michigan State University also produced "considerable agreement between faculty and student affairs workers as to which educational outcomes are important to the purpose of higher education" (Hintz and Stamatokos, 1978, 151). Neither group, however, perceived a high degree of cooperation between faculty and student affairs educators nor did they report readiness for greater interaction in meeting educational outcomes. Thus, though some appreciation for a developmental approach to the learning process in college is shared by both student affairs educators and faculty, systematic educational strategies that might be employed by both groups must still be identified and implemented. The mentoring relationship is one such role. At the University of Nebraska, for example, the Student Development

Mentoring-Transcript Project utilizes six major dimensions of human growth and understanding to guide a holistic approach for mentor-student relationships:

1. *Personal identity and lifestyle:* sense of purpose, personal value systems, career planning, self-assessment and goal-setting skills, decision-making and problem-solving skills.

2. *Interpersonal competencies and relationships:* communication skills, ability to understand and empathize, capacity to assist and provide emotional support, group work, leadership skills.

3. *Academic skills and intellectual competencies:* ability to participate in independent learning, use successful study skills, cognitive growth through structured learning experiences, master specific vocational skills.

4. *Aesthetic awareness:* appreciation of the arts including music, art, and literature; a sense of personal competency and participation in the arts.

5. *Health, physical fitness, and recreation:* knowledge of health, fitness, and nutritional information; recreational, athletic, and leisure skills.

6. *Multicultural awareness:* sensitivity and understanding of the diversity of values, perspectives, and lifestyles of different cultures ability to interact effectively in a pluralistic society.

Mentoring Relationships

The term *mentor* has its derivation in Homer's *The Odyssey* in which the character Mentor was entrusted with the care and education of Telemachus while his father, Odysseus, was away fighting in the Trojan War. The mentoring relationship has recently become one of the latest "buzz words" within the corporate world and professional groups as well as postsecondary education. Much of this attention can be attributed to the research conducted by Levinson (1978) regarding the stages of adult development. He found that young adults, approximately seventeen to twenty-two years of age, enhanced their development through temporary mentoring relationships with older adults. Mentors performed a number of functions including the roles of teacher, counselor, guide, sponsor, and exemplar. Thus, the younger adult or protege not only learned specific vocational and educational skills but also was introduced and initiated to the adult world through the efforts of a mentor acting as a friend who took a personal interest in facilitating the younger person's growth and advancement. Levinson (1978) described the mentor as a "transitional figure" who functioned precariously as a mixture of parent and peer while not becoming too much of either. Because mentors exemplify qualities that the younger person is striving to attain, their values, virtues, and accomplishments are internalized by the protege and are reinforced through mutual love, admiration, and encouragement.

Mentoring in the Corporate World. In a survey study of 1,250 successful business executives, Roche (1979) found "nearly two thirds of the respondents having had a mentor or sponsor, and one third of them has had two or more mentors" (p. 14). Those with a mentoring relationship earned larger salaries, engaged in more formal education, and were more likely to follow a systematic career path. They were also happier with their careers and derived more satisfaction from their work. Hennig and Jardim (1977) found that successful women in business also attributed much of their achievement to having a mentor or "father-like sponsor" who assisted them in their careers. These findings have influenced some businesses to incorporate a systematic mentoring system that provides young employees with an assigned sponsor (Harvard Business Review, 1978) and has resulted in a growing awareness that women must make a special effort to find sponsors as well as be willing to act as mentors for their younger female colleagues (Business Week, 1978; and Shapiro and others, 1978).

Mentoring in Postsecondary Education. As noted earlier, the quality and quantity of faculty-student relationships have traditionally not fulfilled their potential impact on the learning process in college. In their chapter in *The Modern American College,* Gaff and Gaff (1981) recently reflected on this issue:

> The research on student development suggests that it may be necessary to find more areas for faculty-student interaction, beyond the traditional arenas of the classroom and professor's office. Contact in these settings has a purposeful, task-oriented quality that formalizes interaction and precludes much of the human drama that can stimulate growth. Additional opportunities for exploring ideas and values important to student development are needed [pp. 652–653].

At the same time, Pascarella and Terenzini (1978) concluded that a high degree of interaction with faculty members during the freshman year may influence student expectations and, thus, produce more faculty-student relationships during future years. Finally, Katz (1979) expressed concern regarding ways in which postsecondary education has "neglected students" in recent years as compared to the decade of the 1960s. "It is one of the ironies of higher education that student interests and needs were most considered when students were actively demonstrating. Even educators seem to need political prods in order to do more adequately what one would think is one of their central functions: to serve student development" (Katz, 1979, p. 34). We contend that systematically arranged mentoring relationships between students and educators can help to humanize the college experience and alleviate some of these critical concerns and issues.

Cross (1976) reviewed the skill classifications in the *Dictionary of Occupational Titles* and noted that mentoring was listed as the most complex role in terms of required interpersonal skills. It is listed above negotiating, instructing, and supervising in that order. Table 2, modified from Breen and others (1975), provides comparative descriptive statements which relate to

Table 2. Some Descriptions for Roles that Require Interpersonal Skills

Instructing

- Listens to opinions and ideas
- Presents lectures
- Elicits and discusses theories and practices
- Trains others in effective and cognitive principles
- Uses demonstration and role-playing techniques to teach subject matter
- Conducts seminars and workshops
- Illustrates theories and principles through explanation and example
- Tests and assesses knowledge and understanding of the problem-solving process
- Answers questions
- Points out similarities and differences of viewpoints
- Makes inferences about the cognitive behaviors of others

Consulting

- Gives information and ideas based on experience and training
- Recommends content and methods of training
- Provides sources of technical information
- Gives ideas to define and clarify procedures and product specifications
- Informs on details of working out objectives
- Gives advice
- Explains content of programs
- Assists in working out of plans
- Guides implementation of plans
- Meets with, listens, discusses, and answers questions to resolve problems and promote cooperation
- Makes suggestions to reduce resistance and sharpen understanding of program goals
- Recommends alternative courses of action

Mentoring

- Listens
- Asks questions
- Reflects back feeling and informational responses
- Guides conversation
- Diagnoses and evaluates feelings and information
- Feeds back diagnoses
- Makes suggestions
- Prescribes treatments and approaches to solving problems
- Instructs: presents information, explains, gives examples
- Forecasts possible outcomes, predicts consequences of alternative courses of action
- Motivates
- Persuades and influences in favor of a point of view
- Provides feedback and evaluation of progress
- Makes new suggestions based on new information or circumstances

Source: Breen, P., Donlon, T., and Whitaker, U. *The Learning and Assessment of Interpersonal Skills.*

the roles of instructing, consulting, and mentoring. Descriptive words relating to instruction tend to be prescriptive (presents, elicits, trains, conducts, and tests) while the descriptors for consulting are more facilitative (recommends, explains, assists, guides, and listens). The role of mentoring includes both facilitative and prescriptive functions, encompassing a broader educational relationship with students which transcends both cognitive and affective educational variables. Thus, as Cross (1976) noted, "Mentoring involves dealing with individuals in terms of their total personality in order to advise, counsel and/or guide them, and this seems a necessary interpersonal skill for many college faculty members today" (p. 205). Lester and Johnson (1981) also recognized the total nature of mentoring relationships in their definition:

> Mentoring as a function of educational institutions can be defined as a one-to-one learning relationship between an older person and a younger person that is based on modeling behavior and extended dialogue between them. Mentoring is a way of individualizing a student's education by allowing or encouraging the student to connect with a college staff member who is experienced in a particular field or set of skills. The relationship has formal and informal aspects. . . . What seems to confirm a mentoring relationship is its informal dimensions, which give greater significance to the contact between the two persons involved. The student must have respect for the mentor as a professional and as a human being who is living a life worthy of that respect. The mentor must care enough about the student to take time to teach, to show, to challenge, and to support. In some elusive fashion, the mentor must embody values, aspirations, wisdom, and strength that the student respects and perhaps wishes to attain as well [pp. 50–51].

Faculty mentors at Empire State College work with students to develop the individualized learning contracts important at this institution. The dean of the Learning Center recently commented on the mentoring role: "It's one thing to teach a class of thirty. But mentoring thirty students under this system requires the faculty member to sit eyeball to eyeball with a serious adult learner. There's no faking it and doing a potted lecture. A few faculty members may experience real stress, and a few may have scurried back to traditional teaching. Yet the rewards along this path are stunning" (Gross, 1976, p. 14). Some authors have maintained that rewards for the mentor have their basis in Erikson's concept of generativity in which the older person fulfills a need for providing guidance and knowledge to be utilized by the next generation (Brown, 1980c; Lester and Johnson, 1981). This need for generativity might be achieved through parent-child, master-apprentice, and teacher-student relationships as well as through the classic mentoring role. At any rate, there are intrinsic rewards for mentors as they contribute to the growth of the younger person just as there are in other traditional "helping" roles (Carkhuff, 1971).

At the University of Nebraska, Brown and others, (1979) asked students to indicate from a list of faculty, student affairs educators, and administrators which individuals might be potential mentors (Table 3). While faculty members, academic advisers, and counseling center staff members received the most support, a relatively high level of acceptance exists for most institutional personnel in the role of mentor. Even graduate students and undergraduate peers received support from over fifty percent of the respondents. It is thus likely that a mentoring program in post-secondary education could use a wide range of professional and para-professional individuals as mentors.

**Table 3. Student Responses Regarding Resource Persons
Appropriate as Advisers/Mentors
in Determination and Evaluation of Developmental Goals**

Faculty and Staff	*Agree*	*Student Responses (N = 1002)* *Uncertain*	*Disagree*
1. Faculty advisers affiliated with individual colleges	76%	12%	12%
2. Dean of students and assistants	39	29	32
3. Campus ministers	49	27	24
4. Undergraduate student peers	52	21	27
5. Director of housing and assistants	19	32	49
6. Graduate students	51	23	26
7. College deans and their assistants	42	29	29
8. Counseling center staff	71	19	10
9. Academic advisers affiliated with advising office	62	24	14
10. Faculty members	74	10	16
11. Residence hall staff	47	26	27
12. Director of student activities and assistants	40	36	24
13. Fraternity and sorority chapter advisers	39	33	28
14. Athletic coaches	45	27	28
15. Multi-cultural affairs staff	30	44	26
16. Greek affairs office staff	16	44	40
17. Military science faculty	25	40	35
18. University administrators	27	32	41

Source: Brown and others, 1979.

Figure 1. Developmental Mentoring-Transcript Process

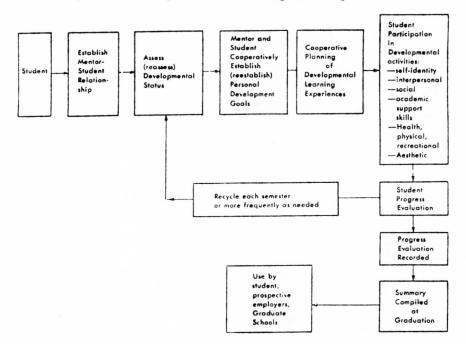

A Systematic Mentoring Process

Figure 1 illustrates a systematic mentoring process which culminates with a student development transcript. This process involves the traditional paradigm of assessment, goal setting, programming, and evaluation in seven distinct phases: (1) establishing the mentor-student relationship, (2) student assessment of their present developmental status, (3) student goal setting, (4) planning appropriate learning experiences, (5) participation in educational and developmental activities, (6) evaluation of progress, and (7) recording of progress in a developmental transcript.

The relationship with the mentor is vital throughout these phases. The focus is on goal setting in developmental areas, but the mentor serves as a consultant-friend rather than a prescriptive programmer. The developmental transcript will be explored fully in Chapter Two and the implementation of the mentoring process is described with some detail in Chapter Three.

Such a mentoring role can enhance the quality of faculty-student relationships in college; provide a proactive, developmental perspective for student affairs educators; and assist in humanizing the general college environment for students.

16

References

Astin, A. W. *Four Critical Years: Effects of College on Beliefs, Attitudes, and Knowledge.* San Francisco: Jossey-Bass, 1977.

Breen, P., Donlon, T., and Whitaker, U. *The Learning and Assessment of Interpersonal Skills: Guidelines for Administrators.* CAEL Working Paper No. 5. Princeton, N.J.: Educational Testing Service, 1975.

Brown, R. D. *Student Development in Tomorrow's Higher Education: A Return to the Academy.* Washington, D.C.: American College Personnel Association, 1972.

Brown, R. D. "Developmental Transcript Mentoring: A Total Approach to Integrating Student Development in the Academy." In D. G. Creamer (Ed.), *Student Development in Higher Education.* Cincinnati: American College Personnel Association, 1980a.

Brown, R. D. "Student Development and the Academy: New Directions and Horizons." In D. A. DeCoster and P. Mable (Eds.), *Personal Education and Community Development in College Residence Halls.* Cincinnati: American College Personnel Association, 1980b.

Brown, R. D. "The Student Development Educator Role." In U. Delworth and G. R. Hanson (Eds.), *Student Services: A Handbook for the Profession.* San Francisco: Jossey-Bass, 1980c.

Brown, R. D., Baier, J. L., Baack, J. E., Wright, D. J., and Sanstead, M. "Implications of Student, Parent, and Administrator Attitudes for Implementing a Student Development Transcript." *Journal of College Student Personnel,* 1979, *20,* 385–392.

Brown, S., and Wood, M. "Faculty and Student Affairs Staff Views of Significance of Educational Outcomes." Unpublished Paper, University of Nebraska, Lincoln 1979.

Business Week. "Women Finally Get Mentors of Their Own." *Business Week,* October 1978, 74–80.

Carkhuff, R. R. *The Development of Human Resources.* New York: Holt, Rinehart and Winston, 1971.

Committee on the Student in Higher Education. *The Student in Higher Education.* New Haven: Hazen Foundation, 1968.

Cross, K. P. *Accent on Learning: Improving Instruction and Reshaping the Curriculum.* San Francisco: Jossey-Bass, 1976.

DeCoster, D. A., and Mable, P. "Interpersonal Relationships." In D. A. DeCoster and P. Mable (Eds.), *New Directions for Student Services: Understanding Today's Students,* no. 16. San Francisco: Jossey-Bass, 1981.

Gaff, G., and Gaff, S. S. "Student-Faculty Relationships." In A. W. Chickering (Ed.), *The Modern American College.* San Francisco: Jossey-Bass, 1981.

Gross, R. *Higher/Wider/Education: A Report on Open Learning.* New York: Ford Foundation, 1976.

Harvard Business Review. "Everyone Who Makes It Has a Mentor." *Harvard Business Review,* July-August 1978, 89–101.

Hennig, M., and Jardim A. *The Managerial Woman.* New York: Doubleday, Anchor Press, 1977.

Hintz, J. A., and Stamatokos, L. C. "Goal Congruence and Perceived Need for Greater Cooperation Between Undergraduate Faculty and Student Affairs Staff." *Journal of College Student Personnel,* 1978, *19,* 146–152.

Katz, J. "Collaboration of Academic Faculty and Student Affairs Professionals for Student Development." In A. C. Tilley, L. T. Benezet, J. Katz, and W. Shanteau (Eds.), *The Student Affairs Dean and the President: Trends in Higher Education,* Ann Arbor: ERIC, Counseling and Personnel Services Clearinghouse, 1979.

Lassegard, R. W. "One Parent's Hopes for His Daughter's Education." *Chronicle of Higher Education,* October 14, 1980, p. 33.

Lester, V., and Johnson, C. "The Learning Dialogue: Mentoring." In J. Fried (Ed.), *New Directions for Student Services: Education for Student Development,* no. 15. San Francisco: Jossey-Bass, 1981.

Levinson, D. J. *The Seasons of a Man's Life.* New York: Knopf, 1978.

Parker, C. A. "With an Eye to the Future. . . ." *Journal of College Student Personnel,* 1973, *14* (3), 195–201.

Pascarella E. T., and Terenzini, P. T. "Patterns of Student-Faculty Informal Interaction Beyond the Classroom and Voluntary Freshman Attrition." *Journal of Higher Education,* 1977, *48,* 540–552.

Pascarella, E. T., and Terenzini, P. T. "Student-Faculty Informal Relationships and Freshman Year Educational Outcomes." *Journal of Educational Research,* 1978, *71,* 183–189.

Roche, G. R. "Much Ado About Mentors." *Harvard Business Review,* January-February 1979, 14–28.

Shapiro, E. C., Haseltine F. P., and Rose, M. P. "Moving Up: Role Models, Mentors, and the Patron System." *Sloan Management Review,* Spring 1978, 51–58.

Steele, M. W. "Correlates of Undergraduate Retention at the University of Miami." *Journal of College Student Personnel,* 1978, *19,* 349–352.

Wilson, R. C., Gaff, J. G., Dienst, E. R., Wood, L., and Bavry, J. L. *College Professors and Their Impact on Students.* New York: Wiley, 1975.

David A. DeCoster is dean of students and associate professor, Department of Educational Psychology and Social Foundations, University of Nebraska-Lincoln.

Robert D. Brown is professor of education, Department of Educational Psychology and Social Foundations, University of Nebraska-Lincoln.

Constructing a developmental transcript stimulates personal growth and the resulting record can be used by students for several productive purposes.

Student Developmental Transcript Systems: An Impetus for Student Growth

Robert D. Brown
David A. DeCoster

Marking progress is a particularly human and a natural phenomena. Parents chronicle their children's height with marks on door jambs and portray other indications of physical maturity with birthday pictures. Cognitive growth, also, is regularly recorded from the moment of baby's first words through college graduation. Grade reports, test scores, and academic transcripts reflect a college's efforts to record cognitive growth, but the markings of growth in other developmental areas are difficult to discern. A person's ability to develop strong interpersonal relationships cannot be indicated by a mark on the wall, nor does a photograph reveal how much insight an individual has about career options.

During college, students grow in their understanding of themselves, their sensitivity to other persons and cultures, their vocational identity, and their interpersonal skills. Colleges hope to promote total student development in these areas as well as cognitive growth, but generally there is no monitoring of progress nor a record comparable to the academic transcript. Although college graduates have their academic transcripts as records of

R. Brown and D. DeCoster (Eds.). *New Directions for Student Services: Mentoring-Transcript Systems for Promoting Student Growth,* no. 19. San Francisco: Jossey-Bass, September 1982.

19

their scholastic accomplishments, they have no counterpart which documents personal growth in other areas.

The developmental transcript system promotes student development in these and other areas through record keeping and documentation of competencies and growth experiences. It can also provide students with a useful record of growth, competencies attained, and accomplishments. The transcript system, when combined with a mentoring relationship, is both a process and a product. The process includes making decisions about developmental goals, determining ways to achieve them, and assessing and reflecting on progress. The product is a record that takes different forms and serves a multitude of purposes.

This chapter describes basic components of a developmental transcript system, the variety of options, and related issues. The discussion includes: (1) purpose and rationale for developmental transcripts, (2) transcript formats, (3) developmental areas, (4) assessment and credentialling, (5) student clientele, and (6) potential levels of support. Institutions and individuals considering a developmental transcript system will need to discuss the relevance of the options, the issues presented, and the implications for implementation on their specific campus.

Purpose for Developmental Transcripts

The purpose of the developmental transcript is to promote student development and there are several reasons it can effectively serve this purpose:(1) Establishment of a developmental transcript system represents an institutional commitment that gives credibility, viability, and intentionality to student development, (2) the process of planning, goal setting, and recording developmental growth facilitates self-awareness, and (3) the transcript record provides documentation that can be used for career advancement. Each of these reasons merits further elaboration and explanation.

Institutional Commitment: Most colleges and universities explicitly support developmental goals in their college catalogues (Bowen, 1977). They allocate money for campus unions, residence hall educational programs, recreational facilities, fine arts programs, speaker programs, and other extra- or co-curricular programs. These activities and programs enrich the campus environment and provide opportunities for students to explore new ideas, become aware of other cultures, and expand their leisure and esthetic interests. At best, these opportunities are viewed as co-curricular, but some administrators view them as supplemental or peripheral to the main mission of the institution. There is little systematic effort to encourage students to pursue developmental goals nor is there any effort to assess or record student accomplishments.

Institutional activities and requirements designed to promote academic and intellectual goals contrast with those available to enhance personal growth (Brown, 1980b). Admissions committees use examination results, high school academic transcripts, and placement examinations for selection, placement, and advising purposes. After admittance, academic advising programs assist students as they register for courses and select academic majors. Student progress is recorded on an academic transcript maintained and secured by the college. Finally, Graduate Record Examinations, senior comprehensives, and other measures are used to assess completion of academic goals.

This assessment, advising, evaluation, and certification process for academic growth is far from perfect, but nevertheless it presents a clear message to students: "We have definite expectations regarding your intellectual development. We believe you should demonstrate that you have breadth and depth by completion of a certain kind and number of courses. We will record your progress, provide advising to assist you in reaching goals, and we expect you to complete specific requirements before awarding you the diploma."

The same message is not apparent to students regarding personal growth in other dimensions. There may be statements in the college catalogue about improving citizenship, gaining cultural awareness, and even enhancing interpersonal skills, but there is neither assessment, advising, and documentation nor an accountability system to describe and evaluate individual or group progress. The indirect message says to students: "We think personal growth is important during college and we provide opportunities for you to pursue your personal development while you are here. We are not willing, however, to devote the thought, time, or budget necessary to assist you systematically in your development. It is more or less up to you to pursue these goals on your own. In the meantime, pass your exams."

As a result of the message about academic goals, faculty and academic officers periodically examine the requirements for their value and relevancy. The entire system is under almost constant review with major changes requiring faculty approval. Students have to take the academic message seriously, as registrars scrupulously review transcripts for accuracy and completeness. Though students sometimes follow requirements grudgingly and faculty often grumble about lack of rigor or breadth, both adhere to the letter, if not the spirit, of the message.

As a result of the message regarding personal development, faculty often see advising as primarily helping students select courses at registration time. Relatively few faculty aggressively seek oportunities to assist students in finding out more about themselves or to engage students in advising relationships that go beyond discussing course selection (Grites, 1979). Faculty involvement in programs fostering personal growth is usually classified as a service activity falling somewhere below research and teaching in the reward structure. As a result of these clear messages, students often make choices that result in postponement of developmental progress. It is primarily through such natural challenges and crises of normal development as being away from home that developmental growth occurs. Academic growth is planned, monitored, and assessed intentionally and systematically. Personal growth in other developmental dimensions is either incidental or accidental.

The concept of a developmental transcript confronts these mixed messages directly and calls for an institutional commitment to foster personal growth much as it does academic growth. Presence of at least the opportunity for students to establish a developmental transcript says something to students and faculty about the relative importance of personal growth. Exact parity between systems designed to promote academic and personal growth may never be accomplished or even be a realistic goal, but a viable developmental transcript option for students provides institutions with a way of putting institutional goal statements into practice.

Record Keeping and Personal Growth. The process of record keeping facilitates personal growth in several ways. The transcript concept implies that, like the academic transcript, there might be certain expected requirements. Just as the student is expected to provide evidence of competencies in math, humanities, or speech for fulfillment of academic requirements, students might also be expected to demonstrate competencies in personal growth dimensions such as interpersonal skills, leadership ability, or development of personal values. Through establishment of expectations, the academic community provides a framework for students to establish academic goals and monitor their progress. Students must match their personal career goals with institutional requirements and arrive at a best fit.

If the institution also expects students to make progess in personal growth dimensions, this impels them to engage in a comparable set of goal-setting tasks relevant to their personal growth. Knowing that a record will be kept and progress monitored encourages students to do serious thinking about goals, time-lines, and strategies. Though it is doubtful a developmental transcript system would ever become as rigid as are many transcript and academic credentialling systems, the presence of even a flexible monitoring system would undoubtedly stimulate students.

Behavior modification research indicates that recording behavior itself strongly reinforces and influences behavior (McFall, 1977). Crossing off tasks from a list of "things-to-do" is a positive experience and provides the individual with a sense of accomplishment, competency, self-sufficiency, and internal control. Many behavioral programs designed for habit change, weight loss, or fitness use record keeping as an integral part of the intervention strategy. In the same fashion, setting goals to become a better group leader and noting incremental progress towards these goals can influence persistence and confidence.

There is also value in recording thoughts and feelings beyond a simple chronicle of accomplishments. Writing, even if to oneself in a diary, can facilitate personal growth. Progoff (1975) has designed a structured and intensive system for using journal writing for personal growth. Participants write about their past, current relationships, and future possibilities. They are encouraged to look for interconnections and to think about what these mean for the future. Progoff describes the process as a loosening up of the "soil of life" that makes all of one's life accessible for use at any time for decision making and thoughts about the future. If the developmental transcript is viewed as a journal of this kind, it is much more than a product. It is an organic process that stimulates, monitors, and records student progress.

Just as the academic transcript is more than a piece of paper, representing a summary of many educational experiences, the developmental transcript can also be more than a record, representing goal-setting, self-monitoring, and recording activities. This record-keeping process is a provocative stimulant to growth.

Career Advancement. The academic transcript serves serveral purposes beyond being an institutional record of an individual student's progress toward fulfillment of degree requirements. It also serves as a credential for entrance into graduate and professional school and is used by employers to screen job applicants. The developmental transcript could be used for similar purposes. Students could voluntarily make their developmental transcripts, or portions of them, available to screening committees or employers.

There is evidence that employers react positively to applicants who have reference letters from faculty who served as developmental transcript mentors. In a study at a career placement center, employment interviewers from eighty companies read a variety of simulated reference letters about job applicants (Pinkney and Brown, 1981). They gave higher ratings to students who were described as having worked systematically on developmental goals in a transcript-mentoring system than to other students equally talented but whose letters included no reference to how the skills were obtained. There is also evidence that employers respond favorably to transcripts that reflect co-curricular achievements. In a national study (Bryan and others, 1981), employers preferred the co-curricular transcript over traditional resumes of a career planning and placement center. Employers also reported wanting to see evidence of competencies gained through participation in co-curricular activities.

These beneficial ratings may be the result of the novelty of the developmental transcript, and if every applicant had a developmental transcript, the benefits might be diminished. Nevertheless, the process of putting together a developmental transcript enables students to have a more accurate picture of their interests and abilities and how these match up with various employer needs. Pilot efforts by the authors to help seniors construct retrospective developmental transcripts indicate students need help in assessing their own development. They find it difficult to determine how various experiences can be translated into marketable skills in the job world.

They need assistance in articulating these skills in interviews with prospective employers. Many seniors think of themselves only in terms of course hours completed or grade point averages. It is difficult for them to translate credit hours and grades into competencies that make them useful to employers. Putting together even a retrospective developmental transcript can be a helpful learning experience for students. The process results in students being better able to articulate who they are to employers and others.

There are undoubtedly other benefits of a developmental transcript system. The worth the transcript system has as evidence of institutional commitment, the value of record keeping itself, and the potential uses for career advancement, however, represent the major purposes and rationale for the transcript system. The relative value of these uses varies from individual to individual and institution to institution, but merit consideration whenever a college or university is considering ways to fulfill its commitment in promoting growth for students.

Transcript Formats

The familiar xerox copy of the academic transcript with its course lists and grades is almost standardized across the country with few exceptions, usually in the form of narrative transcripts. It would be a mistake, certainly at this stage, for the developmental transcript to emulate the restricted format of its academic counterpart. When designing the transcript format, the primary objective is to promote intentional student development and the transcript is an instrumental part of the facilitating process. Because the record itself may have utilitarian value, however, it is also important to consider how well it communicates a student's accomplishments and competencies to others. The transcript may possibly take on several different formats for different purposes and audiences. Formats receiving attention have included: (1) experiential checklists, (2) competency checklists, and (3) portfolios and narratives (Brown and Citrin, 1977).

Experiential Checklist. This transcript format includes a list of experiences related to developmental tasks. These may include activities like: "attended an assertiveness workshop" under interpersonal skill development, "participated in a life planning workshop" or "visited with a career counselor" under career development, "took a moral philosophy class" under moral development, "attended three theatrical productions and discussed the plays with my roommate" under aesthetic development, and "trained for and ran in three fun runs" under physical fitness-recreational development.

The list could be generated in several ways. It could be developed deductively by the mentoring staff with complete lists of activities under each of the developmental areas. The list could be hierarchical, reflecting difficulty or maturational levels within each developmental area. "Reading about careers," for example, would be lower on the developmental task list than "doing an internship in a career area."

Some tasks could encourage breadth as well as depth and these might not fit easily into a hierarchical structure. Attending plays, musicals, and the ballet, for example, might be tasks that broaden a student's exposure to fine arts rather than deepen it. Enhancing survival skills by learning car maintenance and basic cooking skills might be another example of breadth being more important than depth.

The experiential list could be generated jointly by the mentor and student as they decide on goals and determine subtasks related to the goals. Together the mentor and student determine the target goal and outline the activities leading to that goal with the activities constituting the transcript list. Occasionally, the student or the mentor may wish to reorder the list or decide that they wish to work on another dimension for a time.

Students might also choose to record the activities as they are completed, without a preordinate design as to what the activities should be or in what order they should occur. Either alone or jointly with the mentor, the student may set long-range, broad goals with few short-range specific goals. Both the student and the mentor could be alert for relevant activities. This might be especially appropriate for some developmental areas, such as improving relationships with parents.

This activity orientation to development implies that development is achieved by taking direct action, but there is no reason why reflection could not be listed as an activity as well and so recognized by the mentor and student alike. Development is not simply a process of checking off an activities list; it involves thought and deliberation as well. At times the student and mentor might simply note "spent time thinking about career goals" and check it off as a legitimate developmental activity.

Competency Checklist. This transcript format includes a list of attained skills and competencies. The experiential checklist did not address itself directly to skill development. To say that a student "took an assertiveness workshop," for example, does not indicate that the student has become more assertive. The competency list, on the other hand, attests to what students can do rather than the activities or learning experiences they participated in to attain these competencies.

Like the experiential list, the competency list could be developed ahead of time either by the student alone or by the mentor and the student together. The list could be in self-report form or designed to indicate how the competency was obtained and who would certify its attainment. Both the experiential and competency checklists would be organized under various headings that reflect developmental dimensions or areas.

Narratives and Portfolios. These forms of the transcript are more flexible than the checklists. Narrative transcripts could take the form of journal writing mentioned earlier, dialogues between mentor and student, autobiographical statements, or letters of reference. Narrative academic transcripts have met with mixed success (Forrest, 1975). They take time to write and few employers or admissions committees know how to use them appropriately. They could also be time consuming and poorly used, especially if utilized with admissions officers and employers. A summary might be more appropriate for external use. Nevertheless, as a personal record or log to be used by the student alone or in conjunction with the mentor, the narrative form is a viable option for facilitating development.

Portfolios are common resume formats for artists and photographers, and collections of products representing developmental accomplishments can also be envisioned as a record format. Videotapes might demonstrate leadership and speaking skills, newspaper stories might chronicle public accomplishments, and photographs could be used to illustrate and document numerous developmental tasks. Videodisc and videotape technology is becoming increasingly accessible and provides unlimited creative uses for developmental transcripts.

Developmental Areas

Each institution will decide for itself what developmental dimensions it wishes to include and emphasize depending upon the institution's mission and goals for students. Some developmental dimensions may be emphasized in the mentoring process but not recorded on the transcript. There are, however, relatively few variations in the total range of developmental dimensions (Brown, 1980a). The following categories provide a workable framework: 1. *personal identity:* awareness and development of vocational identity, spiritual life, and personal values; 2. *multi-cultural awareness:* sensitivity and understanding of the diversity of values, perspectives, and lifestyles of different cultures; 3. *interpersonal skills:* ability to communicate with others, understand others, and assist others in individual and group settings; 4. *intellectual-academic skills:* competency in writing, speaking, computation, reading, and other skills necessary to succeed in the classroom and continue lifelong learning; 5. *aesthetic development:* appreciation of the performing and fine arts and a sense of competency as a creative person; 6. *healthful lifestyle:* wellness awareness and skills including physical fitness, stress management, and leisure skills. These dimensions can be given different labels and reorganized under different headings to reflect an institutional focus and perspective, but for the most part they constitute the whole person.

Student affairs programming has traditionally focused on interpersonal skill development. Encounter groups, assertiveness training workshops, and leadership training classes are readily available on most campuses. Colleges currently emphasize healthful life-styles through curricular efforts as well as physical fitness and leisure activities. Academic skill training is often available through counseling centers and teaching and learning centers.

Two developmental areas have been neglected in many institutions: moral-ethical and esthetic development. Teaching faculty, student affairs staff, and campus ministers need to attend to moral, ethical, and spiritual development. Disciplinary situations take up time and can be conceptualized and dealt with from a developmental perspective, but more time needs to be given to heightening moral-ethical development. The student who ignores trouble needs help as much as the student who creates trouble.

Aesthetic development is often left up to fine arts course requirements or programs of campus activity centers and unions. Little systematic effort is made to encourage students to participate in cultural activities. Student affairs staffs could enlist faculty and administrative support for cooperative efforts to fill the vacuum in the esthetic area as well as increasing their efforts to work with faculty and campus ministers in promoting moral-ethical development.

The mentoring-transcript system provides the opportunity and the context for the institution to foster development in these neglected areas as well as more traditional developmental areas. The system provides for students examining with mentors their total development and discussing where they are and how they feel about their status. This process means that important developmental areas, not required for academic credentialling, can be given appropriate emphasis and support.

Assessment and Credentialling

Assessment can be informal or formal. It can be done by the student alone as a form of self-assessment, in conjunction with the mentor, by the mentor alone, or through assistance of persons external to the mentor and student. The form and process depends upon the nature of the competency or developmental dimensions being assessed and the intended use of the transcript.

Use of the College Student Development Self-Assessment Inventory (Appendix A) in the mentoring process provides students with a method to look systematically at their total development. It provides a rough, but global, index of where they stand relative to their judgments about themselves. Dialogue with the mentor can provide an external check on the rationale for their self-ratings.

A combination of self-assessment and assessment by and with the mentor is probably even more conducive to growth. If the student's objectives are vague and ill-defined, interaction with the mentor can make them more specific. The mentor can assist the student to identify the step-by-step process and the experiential events needed to reach his or her objectives. The mentor can also assist the student in the search for the meaning and value of steps already taken. The student might record that he or she "visited a career center," "attended an assertiveness workshop," or "gave a public speech to a campus group," but conversations with the mentor could help determine the value of these experiences.

External assessment by someone other than the mentor or the student may be helpful for several reasons. Neither the student nor the mentor may have particular expertise in the developmental dimension being assessed. Assessment of a musical performance, a speech, or a planned personal budget might be more accurately made by someone with specialized knowledge in these areas. Assessment of accomplishments in an assertiveness training or a car maintenance workshop by an expert may also be more convenient and time saving, as well as more appropriate, because of the expertise required.

An assessment center could provide this external assessment as part of a mentoring-transcript system. The center could be used by students and mentors to assist in assessment of skill development and also be tied to a credentialling process. The assessment center might be a consortium of such already available resources on campus as the counseling service, health centers, healthy life-style programs, and teaching and learning centers. The advantage of a central focus, if not a central location, is its consistency with the holistic approach to development. Total assessment before deciding on goals provides student and mentor with a broad picture of current developmental status.

External assessment could be important if the transcript or a portion of it is designed to serve as a credential, that is, certification that an experience occurred or a skill has been attained. External assessment by an expert will generally have more credibility than personal assessment and will be more useful for employment or graduate school purposes.

The importance of self-assessment as a developmental task needs to be considered when thinking about assessment for the developmental transcript. Self-assessment is a lifelong task involving analysis, decision making, and self-discovery. Everyone has to make judgments about his or her skills as they match the talents and interests with those required for success in careers, specific work assignments, and hobbies. During college, students make decisions about career goals, specific course schedules, and their personal life-styles. There are a few opportunities for systematic self-assessment of academic skills, but there are nearly none in other developmental areas. Using external resources for assistance in self-assessment is also a valuable developmental skill. Locating appropriate resources, obtaining feedback, and learning to use feedback are competencies useful throughout life.

Assessment for goal setting, determining progress, and recording purposes need not be viewed as an onerous process, but as a natural and necessary one for personal growth. The mentoring-transcript assessment process can enhance a student's self-assessment skills as well as provide a status and progress report.

Student Clientele

The numbers of students involved in the mentoring-transcript system depend on institutional resources and commitment. The kinds of students depend on institutional and staff philosophies. Expediency may determine initial decisions. Students who volunteer for the program will be the first candidates. Interests of faculty will also be determinants. If an entire department or college makes a commitment to the concept, the students from the respective disciplines will be prime candidates.

Some institutions, however, may explore the question of who should be involved independent of expediency. Very often when personal development programs are offered, those who get involved are already well ahead of others in their development. Assertiveness workshops often attract those already assertive rather than the shy. Encounter groups attract those ready to talk about themselves rather than the inhibited, reading improvement programs enroll the above average reader, and life-planning workshops appeal to those with reasonable career decision-making skills. It is possible that optional developmental transcript programs will attract students highly active in campus affairs and consciously pursuing ways to make themselves more "well-rounded." The narrowly focused student is less likely to participate.

It is too early to say whether a transcript program should be required or in what type of institution required participation would be acceptable and viable. The logistics are difficult and yet Alverno College and Empire State College have developmental goals as integral parts of their graduation requirements and have survived. At larger institutions, group assessment and mentoring might be necessary if all students were involved.

Levels of Support

Two studies indicate there is a core of support for the developmental transcript concept among students, administrators, and parents. The results of a national survey indicate the majority of student affairs officers (63 percent), academic officers (52 percent), and registrars (54 percent) believe progess toward personal growth should be part of a transcript (Brown and others, 1978). Nearly two thirds of each of these groups also believe a developmental transcript could be a worthwhile addition to postsecondary education. In an institutional study, students (65 percent) and parents (66 percent) indicated support for the transcript as a worthwhile addition to postsecondary education (Brown and others, 1979).

Generally, all groups strongly support systematic efforts to promote personal development (85 percent). As indicated, about two thirds of all groups believe a developmental transcript was worthwhile. About half (46 percent) believe personal growth experiences should be available for academic credit and about a third (32 percent) believe progess toward development should be required for graduation. Students (15 percent) were most conservative about requiring progess as a prerequisite for graduation (Brown and others, 1979).

These findings suggest that support exists on most campuses with strong approval for the general concept and a core of support for more specific elements. There is also likely to be a core of dissent which must be recognized in considering a mentoring-transcript program.

Conclusion

The developmental transcript has the potential to be valuable for student development because of the process necessary to produce it and the product itself.

The process provides students with invaluable experiences in self-assessment as well as learning to obtain and use external feedback. The process will also stimulate periods of thoughtful reflection about self, others, goals, and the future.

The product provides the student with a physical manifestation of progress and accomplishments developmentally. As a product it may also be shared with others for use in seeking employment and admission to future education.

References

Bowen, H. R. "College Helps People Discover Themselves." *The Chronicle of Higher Education,* November 21, 1977, p. 9.

Brown, R. D. "Developmental Transcript Mentoring: A Total Approach to Integrating Student Development in the Academy." In D. Creamer (Ed.) *Student Development in Higher Education: Theories, Practices, and Future Directions.* Washington, D.C.: American College Personnel Association, 1980a.

Brown, R. D. "The Student Development Educator Role." In U. Delworth and G. R. Hanson (Eds.), *Student Services: A Handbook for the Profession.* Jossey-Bass, San Francisco, 1980b.

Brown, R. D., Baier, J. L., Baack, J. E., Wright, D. J., and Sanstead, M. "Implications of Student, Parent, and Administrator Attitudes for Implementing a Student Development Transcript." *Journal of College Student Personnel,* 1979, *20* (5), 385–392.

Brown, R. D., and Citrin, R. S. "A Student Development Transcript: Assumptions, Uses, and Formats." *Journal of College Student Personnel,* 1977, *18* (3) 163–168.

Brown, R. D., Citrin, R. S., Pflum, G., and Preston, M. "Is Higher Education Receptive to a Student Development Transcript? A National Survey." *Journal of College Student Personnel,* 1978, *19* (4), 191–198.

Bryan, W. A., Mann, G. T., Nelson, R. B., and North, R. A. "The Co-Curricular Transcript—What Do Employers Think? A National Survey." *National Association of Student Personnel Administrators Journal,* 1981, *9* (1), 29–34.

Forrest, A. "Narrative Transcript: An Overview." *Educational Record,* 1975, *56,* 59–65.

Grites, T. J. *Academic Advising: Getting Us Through the Eighties.* Washington D.C.: American Association for Higher Education, 1979.

McFall, R. M. "Parameters of Self-Monitoring." In R. B. Stuart (Ed.), *Behavioral Self-Management.* New York: Brunner/Mazel, 1977.

Pinkney, J. W., and Brown, R. D. "Contextual Influence on Placement Recommendations: The Developmental Transcript and Causal Attribution." *Journal of College Student Personnel,* 1981, *22* (2), 156–161.

Progoff, I. *At a Journal Workshop.* New York: Dialogue House Library, 1975.

Robert D. Brown is professor of education, Department of Educational Psychology and Social Foundations, University of Nebraska-Lincoln.

David A. DeCoster is dean of students and associate professor, Department of Educational Psychology and Social Foundations, University of Nebraska-Lincoln.

The Mentoring-Transcript Clearinghouse at the University of Nebraska-Lincoln is described and the application of mentoring and transcript concepts in innovative programs are examined.

The National Scene: Other Alternatives and Models

Mary C. Kramer
William A. Bryan
Raymond P. Rood
Martha A. Smith

This chapter describes the Mentoring-Transcript Clearinghouse at the University of Nebraska-Lincoln, and examines the variety of approaches taken by Clearinghouse program contributors to implement the mentoring concept and the co-curricular transcript concept. More complete descriptions of three projects prepared by staff members who participated in the projects at their institutions are also included.

Mentoring-Transcript Clearinghouse

During the spring of 1980, the University of Nebraska-Lincoln established a Mentoring-Transcript Clearinghouse to gather and distribute project descriptions with a resource bibliography of related publications and to establish a network of contact persons at colleges and universities. By July 1981, project descriptions had been received from twenty-four institutions, over seventy publications were listed on the bibliography, and contact people had been identified at approximately two hundred institutions and agencies.

R. Brown and D. DeCoster (Eds.). *New Directions for Student Services: Mentoring-Transcript Systems for Promoting Student Growth,* no. 19. San Francisco: Jossey-Bass, September 1982.

As the mailing list increased, contact persons (see Appendix B) were identified for each of the projects described in the initial mailing and the Clearinghouse continued to distribute composite reports of new projects at the end of each semester. Inquiries for more detailed information or for copies of specific materials were referred directly to the contact person for the respective projects. Institutional representatives were also identified to receive Clearinghouse materials at each institution and agency and to reproduce copies of Clearinghouse updates and distribute them to interested colleagues. Thus, the organization of information and delivery of ideas and approaches to the mentoring and developmental transcript concepts provides participants in the Clearinghouse with options as they plan programs or evaluate those already operational.

The Focus of Program Innovations

The interests of those responding to the Clearinghouse and the focus of the programs submitted for inclusion revolve primarily around one or both of two concepts. The first is the involvement of staff and faculty in taking a holistic approach to their own growth and to involve them in planning and carrying out activities that increase developmental skill levels. The second concept is the creation of a co-curricular, developmental transcript or log by the student, the student and mentor, or institution to record involvement in activities or demonstration of competency in developmental task areas.

Approaches to Mentoring

Projects that unite students with faculty or staff in relationships to encourage and facilitate the holistic growth of the student have evolved from a number of approaches. The variables along which programs differ include:

1. *Mentor selection.* Do the students select mentors or are the students assigned mentors?
2. *Student participation.* Is participation voluntary or compulsory?
3. *Source of mentors.* What campus groups are involved as mentors (faculty, administrators, student affairs staff, academic advisers, upperclassmen)?
4. *Mentor training.* Do mentors participate in training sessions, receive written materials, or work within any guidelines?
5. *Mentor remuneration.* Are mentors compensated by the institution?
6. *Scheduling.* Do students meet with mentors regularly or sporadically? Who initiates contact?
7. *Meeting structure.* Do students and mentors meet in small groups or in individual sessions?

8. *Self-assessment.* Do students use any instruments in assessing current skills and areas for further development?
9. *Limits on participation.* Is the program open to all students or to special groups only?
10. *Focus of program.* What is the focus of the interaction between the mentor and the student? Is the focus set institutionally or mutually by the student and mentor?

Following are descriptions of mentoring programs in which these variables intertwine to produce different composite pictures of mentoring.

Each academic year since the fall of 1979, Andrews University (Michigan) has moved into a new phase of a three-phase Developmental Mentoring-Transcript Project involving faculty and student affairs educators in mentoring relationships with students to assess and plan for the holistic development of students. In Phase I, volunteer mentors were assigned volunteer students. These pairs examined and helped evaluate the dynamics of a mentoring relationship and the student use of a self-assessment instrument in identifying areas to address in growth planning. The mentoring focus of Phase II was the preparation of a plan to incorporate use of a self-assessment instrument in areas of personal development as a complement to academic advising for freshmen. The use of the instrument was optional for the academic adviser. Phase III, in progress currently, calls for the implementation of the plan outlined in Phase II, and for allowing the inclusion of the mentoring process as an option for all advisers. Throughout the phases, mentors attended a preservice training session to clarify the role and function of mentors.

The Model for Student Development at Notre Dame College of Ohio calls for student growth in six developmental dimensions: competence, awareness, autonomy, purpose, integrity, and witness. Students in the class of 1983 began following the model during their freshman year, although upperclassmen could also participate. Each student selected and met with a mentor individually and in small groups. The mentors attended a workshop and received a mentor handbook focusing on communication and interpersonal skills as part of their preparation. The mentor and student worked to involve the student in classes and activities that promote growth in each of the dimensions for development.

At Michigan State University, students and mentors volunteer for the Lifeline program. Using a skills inventory and the Student Development Task Inventory (Prince and others, 1974), the student and mentor assess the student's current skill level and clarify tentative plans. The student and mentor then collaborate on a growth contract (lifeline) to set goals, outline steps to follow to meet the goals, and identify resources that may aid the student in meeting the goals. As this project gets established, training for the mentors, who come from faculty and student affairs ranks, will be minimal, consisting of a brief orientation.

The Faculty Mentor Project at the University of Wisconsin-Madison matches volunteer faculty and volunteer new minority and transfer students for one-on-one interaction during the student's initial year on campus. In this program, the focus is on using the mentoring relationship to provide the student with information about campus and community resources, strategies for receiving help from professors and teaching assistants, and knowledge on how the university system functions. The relationship can also be a forum in which friendship can be explored and the student can talk over feelings and concerns. The mentor and student participants agree to at least three contacts each semester during the year.

Students and mentors also volunteer for involvement in the Mentoring Program at Canisius College (New York). Rather than meeting one-on-one, the mentoring interactions in this program occur in groups of eight students. In addition to the faculty, administrator, or student affairs staff mentor, each group is assigned an upperclass student to assist group discussion and process facilitation. After the first year (1980–1981) in which one half of all new students participated in the program, a campus report noted that participation in a mentoring group had a positive impact on grades and on retention compared to new students who did not participate.

In the third year of implementation, the Student Development Portfolio at Westmont College (California) students take a course, Maturing Theory and Practice, to identify developmental needs, prepare growth contracts and involve themselves in coursework and activities in support of meeting their developmental goals. The class meets in a group four times and the students meet individually with a mentor four times. Participants take assessment inventories and tests and use the results to help in designing an educational program that includes an academic component but focuses on self-understanding and personal development.

Transcript Alternatives

Recording student growth beyond the traditional academic transcript evolves around such issues as:
1. *Storage and distribution.* What campus office manages the collection, storage and distribution of a developmental transcript?
2. *Format.* Does the student or the institution design the transcript format? Is it a narrative, a checklist, or open-ended categories?
3. *Validation.* Does the institution validate the student growth record or is the record an unevaluated self-report?
4. *Measurement criteria.* Is the transcript a list of activities or of demonstrated competencies?
5. *Use.* Is the transcript a log used solely by the student to track progress and plan future growth or is the student encouraged to create a transcript for submission to graduate or professional schools or to professional employers?

6. *Cost.* How is the supplemental transcript funded?

7. *Participation.* Can students choose to have a co-curricular transcript or is it an institutional requirement? Can all students participate? The transcript projects described below represent a variety of approaches to these issues.

At Alverno College (Wisconsin), the official institutional transcript records courses taken and both credits earned and a list of competencies the student demonstrated by the end of each course in one or more of eight areas. The areas are: communication, analysis, problem solving, valuing in decision making, social interaction, understanding the environment, understanding the contemporary world, and responsiveness to the arts and humanities. When the student graduates, competency has been shown in each of these areas in at least four academic courses. In addition, a narrative evaluation by one of the faculty in the student's major department is part of the student's transcript package. This narrative reflects both the student's special strengths and areas which need further development. When assessment of a competency in one of the eight areas is done outside of a course, an assessment center at the college does the evaluation applying established criteria and standards. Thus, a student could meet part of the requirement to demonstrate skill in problem solving by participating in student government or a student judicial board and have this participation evaluated for inclusion in the transcript.

As part of the three phase Developmental Mentoring-Transcript Project described earlier at Andrews University (Michigan), two dozen seniors put together a developmental transcript during Phase II to use in conjunction with an academic transcript in their job hunt in the spring. In Phase III, three seniors from each academic department developed a transcript that mirrored the student's growth in areas other than academic. A graduate student research project is also gathering data to evaluate the worth of the developmental transcript in the job search of these seniors.

Offered through the Student Services Office at Salem State College (Massachusetts), a Student Activities and Development Record Card System provides students with the opportunity to make entries regarding participation in twelve categories: committees and task forces; campus organizations; student government; student publications; intercollegiate athletics and intramurals; performing groups and performances; volunteer service; peer counseling activities; written and oral publications; workshops, seminars, and special training; college related employment; and honors, awards, and college scholarships. Students may update the record card at the end of each semester. All entries are validated by faculty or staff members. The cards of seniors are moved to the placement center and included in the student's placement file although the record card is only released to graduate or professional programs and to prospective employers with the student's authorization.

The Student Involvement Record at the University of Wisconsin-Stevens Point is a four-part document that verifies the student's participation in four areas of co-curricular activity: leadership and managerial training; service or learning involvement; on-campus work experiences; and honors and awards. As the student's involvement in service and learning activities is recorded, the student's participation is evaluated on two dimensions: Class is rated to determine the degree of responsibility; and level is rated to determine the difficulty of the task. Managed through the student activities office, the transcript is distributed only when the student's release is obtained.

Using a portfolio as a job-getting tool is also one of the goals of the supplemental record of nonacademic growth at Notre Dame College of Ohio. The portfolio is constructed by the student and mentor and is a repository of material the student can use to plan goals and to document growth. The portfolio may contain information like personal growth contracts, descriptions of significant college experiences, class projects, and the student's senior project.

Students are encouraged to update quarterly the Student Development Transcript at the University of Minnesota Technical College. Both the activity and the participation level in out-of-the-classroom educational activities are recorded. The evaluation of the student's participation level is made by an employer, adviser, team coach, committee chairperson, or an organizational officer. The student can choose whether to maintain a developmental transcript at this two-year institution.

The Student Activities Involvement Log (S.A.I.L.) (Knefelkamp, 1980) is available to students at the University of Maryland through the office of campus activities. S.A.I.L. is a two-part package. The first part is a folder that explains the purpose of the program, lists sample activities, and gives instructions on the use of the logs. The log forms constitute the second part of the S.A.I.L. package. As a student records an out-of-the-classroom activity, with or without the involvement of a faculty or staff mentor, the student defines the personal impact of the activity by analyzing the experience according to seven skill areas (intellectual, values, personal, interpersonal, career, leisure, and physical). Students record how the activity affected learning skills or how they used skills in each of the areas of development.

At the cost of one dollar a year, the students at the University of Iowa can keep a Student Activities Transcript, illustrating co-curricular activities, on file with the university. The student may obtain copies to send to other educational institutions or to employers at any time, although the university does not mail the transcript for the student. The veracity of the record is not validated by institution, rather, the computer printout of the activities transcript reflects the student's self-report, just as a resume does. Students fill out a scan sheet to record leadership activities, management experiences, awards and honors, community service, and training programs in the development of student organizations and in personal growth.

Another program that structures the student's work with an adviser to plan, accomplish, and log nonacademic growth is the COMPASS (Comprehensive Advising System for Students) at Pine Manor College (Massachusetts). The student and adviser use a Master Advising Portfolio (MAP), containing information about growth skills like decision making and goal setting; campus resource information; and log forms on which the student can reflect on current skills and plan for growth experiences. By completing logs, the student keeps a record of goal accomplishment and activity participation.

There are two more extracurricular transcript options among the Mentoring-Transcript Clearinghouse project descriptions that provide students with a record complementing an academic transcript: the Educational Testing Service's Passport program and the American College Testing Program's National Registry for Continuing Education. The management of continuing education records is the primary goal of Passport. The student is responsible for the authenticity of the documentation of individual educational and vocational credentials recorded on microfiche. The centralization of continuing education records and vocational credentials gives the student a permanent record of learning and work experiences beyond a degree. The student contracts directly with the Educational Testing Service to participate in the Passport program.

The National Registry for Continuing Education offered by the American College Testing Program is a record-keeping and transcript service subscribed to by accredited educational institutions for students who participate in noncredit continuing educational courses. The student receives a confirmation card from the Registry at the end of each course and can order a transcript of all courses on file, including a description of the educational activity. If the student participates in a variety of continuing education courses at many institutions, all of whom utilize the Registry, a complete and permanent record will be available for potential employers.

Uses of the transcript are still being explored. The value of the transcript as a catalyst to holistic advising, to skill identification, and to placement is clear. Other uses may include the use of information about the role of activities in recruiting students, the role of activity involvement in retention, the role of experiences in investigating possible career areas, and the impact of research on student involvement in institutional planning for efficient resource management.

Innovative Programs

The rest of this chapter contains descriptions of three unique programs which blend different methodologies in support of the wholistic growth of students during their college experience and the documentation of this growth for personal recall or in support of the student's candidacy for work or further academic study. Raymond P. Rood shares the approach taken at Azusa Pacific University (California) to assist students in identifying and nurturing internal strength, which is the cornerstone to self-directed personal autonomy, until it develops into the outreach for personal growth. Martha A. Smith describes an institutional commitment to holistic growth for students in the context of a college program that values both the academic and personal development of students at the College of Saint Teresa (Minnesota), where the emergence of the self-motivated learner is fostered and documented. Finally, a unique program at the University of North Dakota is presented by William A. Bryan. In response to the positive evaluation of sample co-curricular transcripts by employers and with the financial support of student government, the University of North Dakota implemented a program involving the student in the examination of non-academic learning and fostering a more balanced value for both academic and nonacademic growth experience.

The Passages Program of Azusa Pacific University

History and Development. The Passages Program is a comprehensive four-year, ten-credit-hour process to help the student understand, use, and integrate the personal development and academic learning that emerges during their undergraduate educational experience. More specifically, Passages assists the student in learning how to (1) explore and identify inner resources, (2) plan and direct individual growth and development, and (3) develop a strategy that enables him or her to become a lifelong learner who can not only survive but lead in the changing world of tomorrow.

The philosophy of the Passages Program evolved from the University's model for training student peer counselors called "Walkabout," which was initiated in 1975. "Walkabout" is the rite of passage experience of most Australian aborigine tribes and involves six to eighteen months of endurance and survival in the Australian outback. It was an article entitled "Walkabout: Searching for the Right of Passage from Childhood and School" (Gibbons, 1974) that challenged the Student Development Department of Azusa Pacific to adapt the "Walkabout" model to their peer counseling internship program while integrating the various elements of this primitive learning model with current development theory, especially the seven vector psychosocial model of Chickering (1969).

The elements identified by Gibbons were: (1) logical inquiry: a challenge to explore one's curiosity, to formulate a question or problem of personal importance, and to pursue an answer or solution systematically and, wherever appropriate by investigation; (2) practical skill: a challenge to explore a utilitarian activity, to learn the knowledge and skills necessary to work in that field, and to produce something of use; (3) service: a challenge to identify a human need for assistance and provide it, that is, to express caring without expectation of reward; (4) adventure/risk: a challenge to the student's daring, endurance, and skill in an unfamiliar environment; and (5) creativity: a challenge to explore, cultivate, and express his or her own imagination in some aesthetically pleasing form. Based upon further study, the element of celebration was identified: the opportunity to share the significant experiences of one's learning experience with intimates in a setting of joy and merriment.

Using the holistic approach of the Walkabout model, the Passages Program became available to the new students entering the University in the fall of 1979. The Passages Program conceives of college as a four-year walkabout or passage that can, if properly explained and structured, become a lifelong transforming personal experience for every graduate.

Program Description. The Passages Program is comprised of six inter-related modules each of which can be experienced as single entities, depending upon the student's developmental readiness and need. Only the Introduction and Orientation phases are required for all students. Each module is related to both an aspect of the Walkabout model as well as to one or more of Chickering's seven vectors.

1. *Introduction:* Students are introduced to the idea of college being a passage during the admission process. Applicants to the university must identify and express what they want from their college experience in three goal statements.

2. *Orientation:* A one-unit nine-week course (Personal Development and the College Experience) is required of all entering freshmen. This general education course involves a three-day orientation session before the first semester as well as eight weeks of small group meetings. In the small groups, under the direction of upperclass group leaders, students explore the concept of individual growth as the focus of college and the purpose of a liberal arts curriculum.

Walkabout component: adventure/risk
Chickering vectors: Development of autonomy, managing emotions

3. *Personal functioning:* A three-unit course (Seminar in Personal Functioning), offered in the spring semester, is primarily for the freshmen who have chosen to become intentional agents in their own growth and development. It is designed to provide the structural challenges and emotional resources for students to move beyond the stage of orientation into the stage of intentional exploration. An experiential foundation is established through a backpacking, rock-climbing, or inner-city project during which students are introduced in an experiential manner to the Walkabout components. Class projects center around self-assessment and problem solving. The challenge of growth planning and the selection of a mentor is undertaken during the final third of the course and students also begin to develop individualized portfolios of their college experience.

Walkabout component: development of practical skills
Chickering vector: development of autonomy, managing emotions, establishing identity, developing competence

4. *Interpersonal relations:* A one-unit semester-long course (Seminar in Interpersonal Relations) provides an opportunity for students to explore interpersonal relations and to develop competencies within their own residence community. The course is designed to focus on how students can become more involved with others and how relating to others contributes to establishing identity. This course can be taken up to three times due to the fact that each residence community offers a unique one-unit course.

Walkabout component: service to others
Chickering vector: developing competence (interpersonal relations), freeing interpersonal relations

5. *Career and life planning:* A three-unit course (Career and Life Planning), available to juniors and seniors, introduces advanced career and life-planning concepts. The students begin to apply what they know about who they are to their upcoming job search and lifelong career and personal planning. An introductory one-unit module is also available, which establishes a philosophic and practical foundation for a liberal arts curriculum.

Walkabout component: logical inquiry, adventure/risk
Chickering vector: clarifying purpose, establishing identity

6. *Celebration:* The students present highlights of their portfolios, including a senior project, to mentor(s), selected faculty, and fellow students along with such other intimates as family members. This sharing and celebration of their journey includes the present focus of their individual passage and their plans for the future.

Walkabout component: celebration, logical inquiry, adventure/risk, creativity
Chickering vector: clarifying purpose, developing integrity, freeing interpersonal relations

Conclusion. The Passages Program is a structured attempt to bring all students to a level of personal awareness and a sense of ownership regarding their college experience that only a minority of college students have experienced, namely, how to learn, how to identify needs, how to locate resources, how to solve problems, how to set realistic goals, and how to take responsibility for one's own life. Azusa Pacific University calls this process "wise travel" and believes it can best be experienced and developed in the context of a liberal arts curriculum. It is hoped that this learning will no longer emerge in spite of how college life is structured, but rather, because of how intentionally it is structured.

The Developmental Objective/Transcript Program

The College of Saint Teresa in Winona, Minnesota, is a small, residential, Catholic college for women offering programs in the liberal arts and professions. The Developmental Objective/Transcript Program (DOT) was developed at the College of Saint Teresa (CST) within the context of a model blending liberal education and student development. With funds provided by the Northwest Area Foundation of Saint Paul, college administrators, staff, and faculty developed the educational model directed at more than thirty specific student outcomes called the "desirable characteristics of a liberally educated person." These characteristics are clustered in the three broad categories of intellectual competence, personal and interpersonal development, and value development. The major thrust of the model of liberal education and student development is to provide a holistic and integrated educational experience for students—holistic because it addresses total human development and integrated because it draws upon all learning experiences, both curricular and co-curricular.

DOT's first thrust enables students to exercise responsibility for planning and directing their own growth. The second thrust encourages students to seek ways of documenting that growth, specifically in areas extending beyond the formal classroom learning experience.

The primary thrust takes the form of personal growth projects consisting of five steps: (1) assessment, (2) objectives, (3) strategies, (4) implementation, and (5) assessment,. With completion of step five, the student is ready to start again on another growth project.

During the initial assessment period, the student has access to the results of the Watson-Glaser Critical Thinking Appraisal and the Student Development Task Inventory giving her an indication of her status in the first two areas of the desirable characteristics: intellectual competence and personal/interpersonal development. Both of these standardized instruments are administered to all freshmen.

Once the student has completed the assessment, she is in a position to indicate areas in which she would like to pursue further development. Included in her DOT package is a "Contract with Self for a Development Project" which asks the student to respond to items related to each of the five steps in the process of formulating a growth project. Samples of completed contracts for personal growth projects are also included in the DOT packet of materials.

After the student has identified the specific behaviors she would like to develop, she then describes a plan of action. Consistent with the educational model at CST, the student is encouraged to consider *all* learning opportunities, both formal and informal, in developing her action plan. An exhaustive list of opportunities for development including clubs, committees, student organizations, elected positions, volunteer services, student work experiences, and student governance is included in the packet, as well as sample action plans for each of the three major clusters using both academic and nonacademic experiences.

The student moves into the implementation stage when she identifies the "what-when-where" elements of her action plan. Course listings, descriptions of specific student services, and the master calendar of college and community programs and activities are useful in this planning.

The assessment of development occurs as the student responds to the final item on her personal growth contract: "indications that I am growing toward my desired outcome." The indications of growth are personal, individualized, and usually unique measures of achievement. Generally, they are formative rather than summative in nature. Students are encouraged to describe the measures or indications of skill as specifically and concretely as possible.

Throughout the entire process of formulating and completing a personal growth project, students have the option of selecting a mentor, utilizing resource persons, or working completely on their own. If a student chooses a mentor, the relationship is generally on a long-term basis, that is, over a minimum period of one year. Mentors may or may not be the student's academic adviser. The choice is the student's.

Students also have the option of choosing resource persons and may choose different resource persons for each personal growth project or different resource persons for various aspects of the same growth project. As another option, students may choose to complete all steps of the process on their own. All options are available and the student has complete control.

The documentation or transcript thrust of the DOT takes the form of a portfolio consisting of a student activities profile, the contracts for personal growth projects, and the developmental transcript. Personal growth projects are summarized and verified by mentors, resource persons, or the student on the Developmental Transcript.

Fifty-five students spread across the four classes volunteered to participate in a pilot project designed to test the DOT process and materials. Most of those students (70 percent) elected to work with a mentor and all but five of the students persisted in the pilot project. Those students who did not persist gave reasons of time pressures. The experience of each of the students who completed the six-month project was documented through structured interviews.

All students who persisted attested to "experiencing growth" in the following areas: (1) increased self-motivation, (2) increased self-awareness, (3) increased self-confidence, (4) increased self-esteem, (5) more relaxed in groups, in prayer, and in other types of reflective self-exploration, and (6) increased awareness and appreciation of nonacademic gifts and abilities.

Mentors were seen as most helpful in assisting students to focus on self-evaluation and on realistic and attainable objectives. Student suggestions for program improvement included providing more examples of action plans, providing more assistance and motivation in getting started with personal growth projects, and providing opportunity for students to meet informally to discuss their growth process and projects.

Students involved in the DOT program have consistently reported personal benefits, but their voluntary efforts in the program often slip to a low priority when ranked with required academic demands. As the CST liberal education evolves with greater refinement, the DOT has tremendous potential for serving as the vehicle through which students unify and integrate their total educational experience. Some discussion has occurred relating to the student portfolio as a graduation requirement. The concept and materials could be introduced in the Introduction to Liberal Studies course required of all freshmen. It could culminate in the Senior Seminar, a synthesizing experience for seniors. As a graduation requirement, the developmental transcript could be incorporated into the student's placement file. Currently, students who voluntarily participate in the program may elect to send copies of their developmental transcript to prospective employers on their own.

The DOT is currently being "tested" by a group of academic advisers as part of a newly developed integrated advising system. Plans for similar use by staff of the student development center are being considered. Results of these efforts will help program directors decide where in the educational model the DOT would best be located.

The University of North Dakota's Co-Curricular Transcript

Discussion of the concept of a Co-Curricular Transcript (CCT) began at the University of North Dakota (UND) in the fall of 1978. Student leaders, staff, and faculty discussed the need to document the various kinds of student learning that occur in an institutional setting beyond that recorded on the traditional academic transcript. Students were enthusiastic about the possibilities and interested in funding such an effort. To determine the efficacy of the project, a national survey (Bryan and others, 1981) was undertaken in the spring of 1980 to seek information from employers regarding the value they would place on a co-curricular transcript as they reviewed potential candidates for positions. Of the 247 employers who responded, seven out of ten indicated they "would definitely want" or "would prefer to have" this type of information included as a part of an applicant's placement credentials. Encouraged by the survey results, the CCT committee proceeded to implement the project.

What Is It? The CCT is a one-page official university document that describes a student's involvement in co-curricular activities while enrolled at UND and can be used also as a supplement to a student's placement or resume file. The program is open to all students on a voluntary basis throughout the year for a one-time registration fee of $5.00. The dean of students office coordinates the project while the basic operating costs for the project are being funded by the UND student government.

A student choosing to participate in this project may indicate involvement in five categories:

1. *Organization activities.* This includes student government, Greek organization participation, association of residence halls, governing councils, student organizations, university committees and taskforces.
2. *Civic activities.* This includes civic organizations, activities, and volunteer work.
3. *Recreational activities.* This includes varsity sports, intramural sports, and tournaments.
4. *Participatory activities.* This includes such things as travel, conferences, conventions, workshops, and university programs.
5. *Awards and recognition.* This includes student government and organizational awards, varsity letters, scholarships, and recreational awards.

The CCT also indicates the level of involvement in the five categories and the years of participation. A CCT master coding booklet (Mann, 1981), which includes a listing of most possible activities within each category, has been developed to assist students and to enable the CCT process to be computerized.

In April of each academic year all registered students are asked to complete a coding sheet indicating all their activities for the year. When the student wants a transcript to be produced, he or she simply requests a final printed copy.

Advantages. The results from the national survey of employers demonstrated the pragmatic advantages of a co-curricular transcript. Employers indicated that they place importance on students' involvement in co-curricular activities and preferred the information contained on a CCT which documented this involvement to that included on a traditional resume of a career planning and placement center. Employers expressed a preference to have a CCT included as part of a job applicant's placement credentials, which supported the premise that such a transcript could have positive effects on the future employability of students.

As the dean of students office works with students developing their co-curricular transcript, staff assist students in assessing their level of involvement in activities and how that involvement enhances their total university experience. The CCT may also aid students as they consider their career goals and how participation in specific activities might augment future careers. The growth of this transcript may lead to more meaningful student participation in campus life as well as in student development itself.

Furthermore, the UND alumni office has expressed interest in

developmental continuum. Development is individualized and unencumbered by age or timing requirements. Thus, each person grows in the same direction, but at varying rates (Knefelkamp and Slepitza, 1979; Rest, 1973).

3. Cognitive development will occur as a function of the person's readiness for change or growth and specific aspects of the person's environment. The environment will thus be perceived as facilitative or inhibitory by virtue of the amount of dissonance seen or felt by the individual. If the person's existing cognitive structural organization cannot incorporate or deal with the varied environmental stimuli, the person will have to stretch her present thinking and discover more useful means for handling her environment.

Further, King (1978) notes that "development proceeds at an irregular rate," as progression from one stage to the next higher stage involves a readiness phase in which the person acquires the "prerequisites" to the next higher level and a phase wherein the person displays the "behaviors characteristic of the next stage functioning" (p. 39). Each individual is seen to extend gradually within-stage "his ability to apply his new capabilities" in an ever-widening circle of "content" areas—a process called "horizontal decalage."

Perry's scheme of intellectual and ethical development consists of nine positions which he groups into four categories:

1. Dualism: Position 1: The student sees "the world in polar terms of we-right-good vs. other-wrong-bad. Right answers for everything exist in the absolute, and are known to authority whose role is to mediate (teach) them" (Perry, 1970, p. 9). Position 2: The student perceives diversity of opinion and uncertainty. She accounts for them as unwarranted confusion in poorly qualified authorities or as mere exercises set by authority "so we can learn to find the Answer for ourselves" (Perry, 1970, p. 9).

2. Multiplicity: Position 3: The student accepts diversity and uncertainty as legitimate but still temporary in areas where Authority "hasn't found the Answer yet" (Perry, 1970, p. 9). Position 4: (a) The student perceives legitimate uncertainty (and therefore diversity of opinion) to be extensive and raises it to the status of an unstructured epistemological realm of its own in which "anyone has a right to his own opinion," a realm which she sets over against authority's realm where right-wrong still prevails, or (b) the student discovers qualitiative contextual relativistic reasoning as a special case of "what they want" within authority's realm (Perry, 1970, p. 9).

3. Relativism: Position 5: The student perceives all knowledge and values (including authority's) as contextual and relativistic and subordinates dualistic right-wrong functions to the status of a special case in context (Perry, 1970, pp. 9–10). Position 6: The student apprehends the necessity of orienting himself in a relativistic world through some form of personal Commitment (as distinct from unquestioned or unconsidered commitment to simple belief in certainty) (Perry, 1970, p. 10).

4. Commitment in relativism: Position 7: The student makes an

initial commitment in some area. Position 8: The student experiences the implications of commitment, and explores the subjective and stylistic issues of responsibility. Position 9: The student experiences the affirmation of identity among multiple responsibilities and realizes Commitment as an ongoing, unfolding activity through which he expresses his life style (Perry, 1970, p. 10).

In these all-too-brief descriptions of Perry's nine positions, the mentor's and mentee's intellectual and ethical positions are to be located. Perry (1981) notes "the development we have traced in college students reveals itself now as 'age-free' " (p. 97). Thus, we can expect the intellectual and ethical development of students, faculty, staff, and administrators to be described by these positions. In the ideal mentoring relationship one might hope the mentor has arrived at and is currently functioning at Position 9, commitment. Thus, the mentor will have achieved a self-created role and be involved in expanding it, know who she is and how she affects other people, places, and things, and be ready to encounter risks to her self-esteem in achieving full potential (Knefelkamp and Slepitza, 1976). Perry's person at Position 9 closely resembles and is complementary to Loevinger's principled autonomous person and Browning's version of Erikson's generative person.

Assuming the mentor is functioning intellectually and ethically from a position involving emerging commitments in her interaction with a variety of potential mentees, she needs to be acutely aware of their relative intellectual and ethical positions or the ways in which such persons derive meaning from their worlds. Perry, in common with other cognitive theorists, postulates that intellectual and ethical growth proceeds most efficaciously when a person is exposed to or stimulated by environmental challenges which are one stage beyond the person's present stage of development. Too much dissonance or challenge would be too great to assimilate. Too little challenge, even with much support, would result in no growth. Indeed, a person may even fixate or stagnate by virtue of the particular mix of challenge and support. For instance, the mentor in dialogue about choosing a major with a mentee who is dualistic in thinking, may prefer speaking about various alternatives, weighing consequences or pros and cons of each possible major, while the mentee wants the mentor simply to tell him, based on the mentor's expertise in these matters, what major to choose. We can anticipate that the mentee will be confused, rather frustrated and possibly angry, and might seek a person who will tell him what to do. A more appropriate mentor response would be to pose perhaps two alternatives, encourage active exploration such as interviewing professors in those majors, and frequent follow-up discussions of the findings from those interviews.

In a situation where there is an inappropriate fit between an assigned mentor and mentee, the mentee might be at a more advanced developmental position than the mentor. In such an instance, the mentor will not be capable of presenting appropriate challenges although she might very well provide encouragement.

If the mentor and mentee happen to be at the same stage of intellectual and ethical development, one might predict they will identify with one another, possibly encourage each other, but there would not be enough dissonance or difference to stimulate or challenge. The question of the mentor as a teacher or guide might be raised in such an instance, as it would arise where the mentee is more advanced in development than the mentor. An exceptional instance in which the mentor at the same developmental level as mentee might serve as a teacher and guide relates to the notion of horizontal decalage. The mentor may have successfully dealt with "content" which the mentee has yet to handle or with which he is currently struggling.

The individual who is at ease with who she is, capable of taking a stand, evaluating her position, and making new commitments when appropriate has much to offer in the mentoring relationship. The flexibility, as opposed to rigid positioning, the willingness to be transparent and open with the mentee, and the recognition that the process of decision making will have to be retraced again and again provide the mentee with a model which can be adapted rather than one which is rigid and unyielding.

Bandura: Social Learning, the Mentor as Model

In analyzing the mentoring relationship, given the unique characteristics of both persons and the nature of their interaction with each other, apparently the mentor occupies a superior position exerting greater impact upon the mentee than vice versa. The mentor appears to be a person worthy of emulation, a person whose behavior, values, attitudes, and thoughts seem attractive and merit imitating.

Bandura's (1971) comments regarding social learning theory generally, and the theoretical construct of modeling in particular, provide further understanding of the mentoring relationship. His conceptions regarding modeling enlighten the nature of the interaction between mentor and mentee. The regular, informal contacts which characterize the mentoring relationship are undoubtedly cemented by generative qualities of the mentor. Through wisely managed dissonance or challenges and judicious support, informal yet intentional teaching and learning occur. The mentor is learning about the varied dimensions of the mentee while the mentee is likely to select and explore those qualities of the mentor which seem most attractive. This exploration and selection process may or may not be a fully conscious effort due to the informality of the relationship. As the relationship deepens and broadens, the mentee can be expected to begin assimilating and accommodating those learnings derived from the mentor and the mentoring relationship. Most learning and mentee behavioral change can be expected to occur by way of the mentor's example, not preachments. If words or lectures about the various areas of student development were most effective in bringing about full student development, then there would be little to recommend extra-class contacts between students and faculty or staff. Yet, as stated in earlier chapters, ratings of faculty as sources of positive influence on intellectual and personal development are positively related to increased commitment to the institution, positive perceptions of the institution, and increased retention (Pascarella and Terenzini, 1976). The basic mentoring relationship certainly would be a significant extra-class contact.

Given an appropriate developmental match in a mentoring relationship, the mentee might be concerned with such matters as developing interpersonal competence and increasing his capacity for intimacy. Such developmental concerns involve the acquisition of complex social skills. Here the mentor as an "exemplar" or model is vitally important and can be immensely helpful. Bandura (1971) notes:

> Under circumstances in which mistakes are costly or dangerous, skillful performances can be established without needless errors by providing competent models who demonstrate the required activities. Where desired forms of behavior can be conveyed only by social cues, modeling is an indispensable aspect of learning [p. 3].

Bandura (1971) defines modeling as subsuming such constructs as imitation and identification and further describes its effects. The three major effects of modeling which vary according to the particular processes involved are:

1. *Observational learning effects,* which are evident when an observer acquires "new patterns of behavior by matching the performance of others" (p. 6) and later reproduces the observed novel responses.

2. *Inhibitory effects,* which are indicated when observers show either decrements in the model class of behavior or a general reduction of responsiveness as a result of seeing the model's behavior produce punishing consequences. Also, *disinhibitory effects,* which are evident when observers increase performance of formerly inhibited behavior after observing models engage in threatening or prohibited activities without adverse consequences (p. 6).

3. *Response facilitation effects,* which are evident by prompting existing behavior and are distinguished from observational learning and disinhibition because no new responses are acquired. Disinhibitory processes are not involved because the behavior in question is socially sanctioned and hence is unencumbered by restraints (pp. 6–7).

Clearly, the mentor's behavioral responses can be expected to have all of these types of effects on the mentee's behavior in various areas of development. Observing the mentor display a sexist attitude with resulting adverse consequences will strengthen the inhibitions of sexist behavior previously learned by the mentee. A mentee who is extremely motivated to conduct original research will be positively facilitated by his mentor's discussions of her efforts in conducting original research. Viewing his mentor in social interaction with her fellow professional colleagues, perhaps resolving a conflict or clarifying an unclear point, provides an excellent opportunity for observational learning for the very quiet, shy, introverted mentee.

By no means is the mentee a passive observer, but rather an active participant whose prior learning experiences, other significant relationships, expectations, values, and such, influence what is learned and not learned.

> In social learning theory observers function as active agents, who transform, classify, and organize modeling stimuli into easily remembered schemes rather than quiescent cameras or tape recorders that simply store isomorphic representations of modeled events [Bandura, 1971, p. 21].

Bandura notes a basic assumption of social learning theory is "that modeling influences operate principally through their informative function, and that observers acquire mainly symbolic representations of modeled events rather than specific stimulus-response associations" (p. 16). Thus, the mentee's learning will be more clearly understood by an examination of subprocesses involved in modeling phenomena: (1) attentional processes, (2) retention processes, (3) motoric reproduction processes, and (4) reinforcement and motivational processes. To derive the greatest degree of benefit from observing the mentor, a mentee will have had to "attend to, recognize, and differentiate the distinctive features of the model's responses" (Bandura, 1971, pp. 16–17). The observer will be motivated to observe closely or ignore a model based on such factors as the motivational and psychological characteristics of the observer, and the physical and acquired distinctiveness of the model as well as his power and interpersonal attractiveness (p. 17). Given the various life concerns of most mentors and mentees, a mentee will have a multitude of opportunities for attending to relevant behaviors—relevant as regards various developmental concerns such as intellectual competence, communication skills, and interpersonal skills.

In learning through observation of the mentor, the mentee does not repeat the model's behavioral responses, but transforms them by using one or both of the representational systems, the imaginal ("enduring retrievable images of modeled sequences of behavior") and verbal ("verbal coding of observed events") (Bandura, 1971, p. 17). Thus, "these memory codes serve as guides for subsequent reproduction of matching responses" (Bandura, 1971, p. 18). In the short run, a mentee will often have occasion to try out a behavior learned from the model in relation to peers, other faculty, and other adult figures in his life, thus giving himself an opportunity for finding out if the response is one that works or not. This trial might also serve as a check of his representational systems.

Motoric reproduction processes involve "the utilization of symbolic representations of modeled patterns to guide overt performances" (Bandura,

1971, p. 22). In the mentoring relationship, many subtle motoric behaviors will be displayed, consciously and unconsciously, by the mentor. If the mentee is predisposed to be sensitive to or aware of such behavior as regards various areas of development, doubtless these processes will be profitably utilized. However, it might be expected for some mentees that the mentor will have to make conscious efforts to point out the need for more attention to the usefulness of such motoric reproduction processes in observational learning. Concerning reinforcement and motivational processes, Bandura says,

> A person may acquire and retain the capacity of skillful execution of modeled behavior, but the learning will rarely be activated into overt performance if negative sanctions or unfavorable incentive conditions obtain [1971, p. 22].

The mentee will be motivated to reproduce modeled behaviors in those developmental areas modeled by the mentor which the mentee has seen praised or somehow positively reinforced. The introverted mentee who has a strong need to belong may attempt to join a professional club, with the knowledge that his mentor did similarly when she was his age.

> Reinforcement variables not only regulate the overt expression of matching behavior, but they can also affect observational learning by exerting selective control over the types of modeled events to which people are most likely to attend. Further, they facilitate selective retention by activating deliberate coding and rehearsal of modeled behaviors that have functional value [Bandura, 1971, pp. 22–23].

For example, a mentee with serious problems in the communication skills area, attracted to an articulate mentor who is in demand as a guest lecturer in his field, will be expected to acquire at least some of the mentor's behaviors. Additionally, the mentee can be expected to pay close attention to the mentor's speaking behavior in further face-to-face or group sessions.

> In the social learning view, modeling stimuli serve more as sources of information than as automatic conditioners. Observers often perform operations on modeling inputs so that transformational and organizational processes are involved as well as associational ones. Less structural correspondence is assumed between memory codes and the original modeled patterns. Verbal representation is assigned a greater response guidance function [Bandura, 1971, p. 25].

The mentee can be expected to mold and integrate observational learnings with his own prior learning through transformation, data reorganization, and relating "new" learnings to "old" learnings, using words to represent those modeled behaviors of the mentor. Possibly, the mentee will discuss the mentor's behaviors with his peers, thus mentally turning those behaviors over in his mind and closely examining them. In so doing the mentee will probably very consciously choose those behaviors which best fit his existing self-concept or which enable him to move toward an idealized self-concept.

Bandura (1971) suggests a mentee will think about his behaviors, imitate certain modeled behaviors, integrate them into his present schema, and not simply mimic his mentor's behaviors. A healthy mentoring relationship would find the mentee learning and reproducing in a selective fashion.

> Model characteristics exert the greatest influence on imitation under conditions in which individuals can observe the model's behavior but not its consequences. When the value of modeled behavior is not revealed, observers must rely on such cues as clothing, linguistic style, general appearance, age, sex, likeableness, and various competence and status symbols as the basis for judging the probable efficacy of the modeled modes of response [Bandura, 1971, p. 55].

In many mentoring relationships, the mentees may not observe their mentors very often outside of their face-to-face meetings; thus, the above observation has particular significance. Indeed, the catalyst for the relationship may be such things as likeableness, clothing, and general appearance. It is also likely to provide a partial explanation for the breakup of mentoring relationships after a certain period. Few people live up to their initial "star" billing, which many freshmen may ascribe to many full-time faculty and staff. Thus, initially the mentee may "buy" and try to "sell" many modeled behaviors of his mentor only to be selectively reinforced by others. Consequently, the mentee can be expected to alter his perception of the mentor's behaviors based on concrete feedback received when he tries to reproduce certain behavioral responses first seen modeled by his mentor.

Thus, viewing the mentor through the theoretical construct of modeling suggests what Pascarella and Terenzini (1976) concluded,

> It would appear that the conception of the faculty member as a role model for students may have both conceptual validity and educational usefulness for those institutions whose educational goals are more broadly conceived than simply the inculcation of knowledge or career preparation [p. 39].

Erikson: The Perfect Mentor—"Generative Man"

Browning (1973) provides a comprehensive picture of the person who has successfully achieved generativity, the major developmental issue of adulthood. "Generativity, then, is primarily the concern for establishing and guiding the next generation" (Erikson, 1968, p. 138). Favorable accomplishments of generativity is predicated on the reasonably successful synthesis of the preceding psychosocial tasks associated with infancy, early childhood, prepuberty, puberty, adolescence, and early adulthood. Each of these psychosocial tasks is relevant to the mentoring relationship.

"Generative man contains within himself a fund of *basic trust* in the world and *hope* for the future" (Browning, 1973, p. 182). Fundamental in the initial stages of the healthy mentoring relationship is a trusting attitude of the mentor toward others. To give oneself or to even approach a student with "pure" motives would seem to be an impossibility without such basic trust. With a firm hope in the future, the mentor finds motivation to proceed in her investment of time, energy, and resources in the mentee.

"Generative man also has the capacity for *autonomy* and the virtue of will. This is to say, he trusts those deeper forces within himself which propel him toward growth and individuation" (Browning, 1973, p. 183). The mentor is thus capable of respecting and trusting his own individuality as well as that of the mentee.

> Generative man seeks a union of mutual recognition and not a union of self-obliteration and self-absorption. Generative man seeks a union of reciprocal patterns of regulation and mutual activation. It is a union that protects his individuality as much as it overcomes his loneliness. It is a union that seeks to "know even as we are known." Generative man seeks a wider and more inclusive union which can give recognition, regulation, and communion to his own inevitable uniqueness [Browning, 1973, p. 184].

In these thoughts, we readily recognize several qualities of the mentoring relationship. Obviously, the mentor and mentee derive much mutual benefit and satisfaction from the mutually respectful relationship. A key aspect of a healthy relationship is the recognition and respect by mentor and mentee of each others' individuality and receptivity to draw from the well of uniqueness as each deems appropriate, while retaining their individuality. The frequency of mentoring relationships lends support to the notion that "generative" persons actively seek such relationships in response to their social needs (to combat loneliness) and desire opportunities for mutual give and take with an ever-widening circle of individuals. Also implicit in these ideas is the notion that a mentor would not encourage a mentee to lose himself in the relationship. Indeed, the clear picture emerges of a moving, growing, dynamic union of two distinct individuals.

The capacity for *initiative* and the virtue of *purpose* derive from the enhanced capacity for autonomy and the virtue of will. "Essentially, man's initiatives aim toward complementarity and not toward domination" (Browning, 1973, p. 185). This quality of complementariness by mentor and mentee seems vital in achieving and maintaining a union characterized by mutual giving. Otherwise, the relationship could easily be a one-sided affair with either mentor or mentee doing all of the giving. Achieving the capacity for initiative involves the acceptance of inherited morality, tempered by certain experiences and shaped by resulting syntheses. Thus, generative man, or the healthy mentor, will express morality, yet "stop short of moralism—those blind and totalistic rejections of all people and experiences which cannot conform to his own customary ways" (Browning, 1973, p. 186). Unquestionably the healthy mentoring relationship would find the mentor openly sharing ideas and opinions from a clearly articulated value framework, yet not imposing those ideas and opinions upon the mentee. Rather, the mentor would respect and accept the values of the mentee. However, in being a guide, the mentor will inevitably be rather persuasive and powerful in influencing the values and morality of the mentee. The mentee can be expected to challenge those expressed and covert values of the mentor, as might also be expected of the mentor.

The generative man has the capacity for *industry* and *competence,* terms which Erikson uses to refer to the "capacity for culturally meaningful work and discipline which builds on but also extends and possibly exceeds the natural inclinations of play" (Browning, 1973, p. 191). Competence is a critical issue for young adults and, thus, building and maintaining a relationship with a mentor who has a clear sense of her own competence in the intellectual, physical, and interpersonal realms will provide an excellent opportunity for guidance on the issue.

Possessing a "viable identity (the question of who one is) and a discernible style of fidelity (the question of whom one can trust)," the generative person "can also present himself as one who can be trusted, just as he can help guide others to their own discovery of that which is worthy of their commitment and loyalty" (Browning, 1973, p. 193). The mentor, who has achieved a "workable" identity and a sense of what is trustworthy in herself and in her life, thus brings to the mentoring relationship a clear, congruent personality which the mentee can quickly experience and derive meaning from in clarifying his own identity. The mentor who is acutely aware of who she is and is quite accepting of and comfortable with herself appears to be capable of freely entering into a mentoring relationship with a trusting rather than a suspicious or defensive stance. This comfort level associated with self-acceptance can encourage a measure of comfort in the mentee, thus enhancing the potential of the mentoring relationship. The mentor who has not achieved a clearcut identity may often bring some identity confusion to the relationship which may cause some difficulty in establishing trust and maintenance of autonomy.

Erikson's next developmental issue, the capacity for *intimacy* and the virtue of *love,* is predicated on the achievement of identity since a person with a clear sense of identity can freely enter close, intense relationships without fear for loss of self. Also, the capacity for intimacy and the virtue of love are seen as "interacting modalities of giving and receiving—that is, of sharing" (Browning, 1973, p. 195). A key aspect of the mentoring relationship by both mentor and mentee is their sharing in the union which fosters and mirrors the level of commitment to the relationship.

The capacity for *generativity* and the accompanying virtue of *care* represent the core qualities of the generative person. This quality of generativity "rests upon and synthesizes all preceding modalities, capacities, and virtues of the earlier stages" (Browning, 1973, p. 195).

The person who has successfully resolved these issues and accomplished these psychosocial tasks will possess those characteristics necessary for nurturing and caring for her successors. She will find the role of mentor to be compatible with her interests in "establishing and guiding the next generation" (Erikson, 1968, p. 138).

Concluding Remarks About the Conceptual Bases

Each mentoring relationship clearly is composed of two principals who enter, change, and exit from the relationship at identifiable levels of intellectual and ethical development. The degree of change which is effected by the relationship is a function of the learning which occurs, for the most part, through effective modeling by the mentor. The mentor is motivated to serve such a modeling role by virtue of her achievement of the stage of generativity and commitment wherein she can have a hand in establishing and guiding the next generation.

Given this conceptual base, it is obvious that the fostering of mentoring relationships between students and faculty, student affairs staff, and administrators is an appropriate and worthy goal for higher education institutions.

Feasibility Issues

In light of the preceding discussion of the mentoring relationship, a number of questions emerge relating to the feasibility of the developmental transcript mentoring system. Is it practical to envision faculty, staff, administrators, and even students, on a selected basis, serving as mentors, generally? Further, is the role of developmental transcript mentor beyond the reasonably expected performance of persons in these professional and preprofessional positions?

Creating an institution-wide program wherein each student is assigned a mentor raises questions regarding the presentation of such a plan to a diverse audience. In addition to the variety of potential mentors, enormous differences will exist in the students. Given the varied stages of development of the diverse student populations found on most campuses, many students might be expected to *not* see the need for a mentor or for a process which focuses on such areas of development as personal identity and life-style, interpersonal relationships, aesthetic development, physical fitness, and multicultural sensitivity and understanding. Such students may be quite mature, with adequate development in such areas, and use other resources outside of the institution for needed support and challenge. With the increasing numbers of adult learners, many of whom work full time and attend school part time, the faculty or other institutional representatives may be seen as secondary sources of influence. Thus a mentoring relationship would have to be forced rather than growing out of an informal or a naturally developing connection or bond. The consequences of such action might work against the development of an effective mentoring relationship if it became institutionalized for all students and faculty or student affairs professionals.

The informal, dynamic nature of mentoring relationships, as seen through Levinson and his associates' work (1978) and as described earlier using the ideas of generativity and modeling, suggests some conflict with a relationship in which the individual mentor assesses formally or informally, advises, evaluates, keeps systematic records, prescribes, and then ultimately certifies. Certainly, a "wise and faithful teacher, guide and friend" will assess when asked, advise when requested, and may even prescribe, fully realizing that such prescription may be accepted or rejected. Yet, the developmental transcript mentor may feel compelled in carrying out her role to advise and prescribe in areas of development within which she is still personally struggling. She may be developmentally "immature," or less mature than her mentee, and therefore a very poor model for her assigned mentee.

The question of ethnic and sexual group membership must be confronted in light of the general composition of the pool of potential developmental transcript mentors. Roughly 75 percent of the faculty in higher education are predominantly white, middle and upper class males. If mentors need to be role models, many ethnic and female students will encounter difficulty in establishing mentoring relationships. Whether dealing with male or female, white or ethnic, graduate or undergraduate, vocationally-oriented or liberal arts-oriented, U.S. or international students, the question of effective models is an important one, assuming all students are to have the opportunity for mentoring relationships. Given the present composition of faculty and staff and dominant social stereotypes and attitudes of most of them, it is doubtful if any students other than middle- and upper-class white males will find ample, willing mentors in today's American colleges and universities. An additional problem exists for those female and ethnic minority faculty, staff, and administrators. They may already be over-burdened with the demands of the institution to provide representation on various committees, subgroups, or other assignments where their point of view is needed. Problems of perception also abound, with students holding certain myths, biases, and reservations regarding the white male faculty, and faculty possibly holding restrictive attitudes towards various ethnic groups and females. Such attitudes would undoubtedly impinge on the development of a reciprocally beneficial arrangement and pose a serious limitation. Then, there is the question of mentors for those students from other countries whose cultural values differ from Western norms. How does a mentor for such a student serve fully the mentoring role and cope with the complex problems of facilitating growth and development which will be congruent with that person's reentry to his culture?

Sexual harassment presents another potential trap for cross gender mentoring relationships. Women students have long complained about demands made by male professors; and the mentor-mentee relationship provides a climate in which such intimidation can flourish if the motivation is not genuine interest in helping students achieve their goals. A clear understanding of the roles implicit in mentoring may help prevent the occurrence of this problem.

A related feasibility issue concerns "goodness of fit" in the matching process. If the institution is committed to utilizing a mentoring program, then each student is entitled to a mentor. Since the relationship is of such a personal nature, what happens to the student whom no one wishes to mentor? Personality or physical characteristics may make a student unattractive as a choice; by the same token, the opposite might be true, and a student might be chosen for the wrong reasons. The mutual selection process under which mentoring seems to flourish may be lost when the program is institutionalized. The question of what happens when a student requests a mentor who does not want to play that role for that particular student may be difficult to decide. Additionally, charges of favoritism may be difficult to quell if unequal treatment exists.

The question of healthy, functioning mentors and their working climate arises in light of the observation, derived from Perry and other cognitive developmental theorists, that developmental growth can be facilitated by requisite support and challenge. What happens to the person functioning at a particular level of psychosocial or intellectual and ethical development when the challenges are many and the needed support is felt to be lacking? The theorists suggest that the person may retreat to a lower level of functioning for survival purposes. Thus, institutional climates may facilitate or preclude the development of mentoring relationships. If professors are encouraged to do research and write as opposed to forming meaningful relationships with students, then the likelihood of such a program flourishing is minimal. Additionally, the institution may, in fact, encourage the professor or staff member's functioning at a lower level developmentally than the mentor role demands. If institutional policies and practices thwart the intellectual and personal development of faculty and student affairs professionals, there is little chance that those persons will arrive at the stage required for providing a collaborative, trusting relationship with students. Institutions which operate in ways which indicate a lack of trust of the faculty or staff member, which do not include the faculty or staff in the decision-making process, or do not reward creative or innovative activities may contribute nothing to the continued growth and development of those persons. Additionally, it is possible to have faculty members or staff personnel who are at one level of development in one area such as the intellectual or cognitive domain, and be at a quite different level in some other area. Thus, some of the goals of the mentor-mentee relationship could not be attained due to the inability of the mentor to function effectively in providing the challenges and supports necessary for growth. In some instances the mentor may actually be dependent upon the mentee, resulting in exploitation and manipulation.

The training and evaluation of mentors pose some interesting areas for investigation. The present status of faculty advising points up some of the difficulties which are inherent in an approach such as mentoring. Few faculty members have had the training in the helping skills required to perform the advising role beyond the course selection and class scheduling level. Much more complex skills are needed if the mentoring process is to be successful; yet the time and resources for developing these skills are not available. Additionally, the role and training of most student personnel services workers has not been compatible with the expectations of the mentor. Few have expertise in assisting in the assessment of the development level of students, nor are they skilled in prescribing specific activities designed to foster individual development and growth. Their approach has been much more programmatic, with the possible exception of counseling programs, where the focus is on the group rather than the individual.

The evaluation of individual mentors and the mentor program is fraught with difficulties. Does the "success" of the student while on the campus or after graduation figure in the "success" of the mentor? Does the student evaluate the mentor, in the same way students evaluate professors? Does the institution evaluate the individuals and the program as well? Is the number of student requests for a given mentor indicative of her effectiveness? How does the person's evaluation as a mentor figure in the reward process? These and other related questions pose problems for the institution which undertakes a complex task such as providing developmental transcript mentors for students.

Conclusion

There is no question that the mentoring relationship furnishes tremendous opportunities for learning and growth. There is also no doubt that there exists an adequate theoretical basis to support the existence of such an arrangement. Given the purpose of colleges and universities to promote individual development, it follows that the campus setting provides the perfect environment in which the mentoring relationship can flourish. There must, however, be sufficient commitment on the part of the institution to the idea that the benefits to be derived are worth the time and effort involved in the professional development and evaluation activities which would be required.

The preceding discussion has presented psychosocial, cognitive-developmental, and behavioral theories which provide sound rationale for the use of mentors in the educational setting. The management issues involved in developing and implementing a formal program using developmental transcript mentors pose formidable, but not insurmountable, obstacles. Commitment to the fullest possible growth and development of every student in all areas of life forces institutions to search for ways to insure maximum interaction between faculty and students. This intentional interaction could be the outcome of the developmental transcript mentor program.

References

Bandura, A. (Ed.) *Psychological Modeling: Conflicting Theories.* Chicago: Aldine-Atherton, 1971.

Browning, D. S. *Generative Man: Psychoanalysis Perspectives.* Philadelphia: Westminster, 1973.

Erikson, E. *Identity: Youth and Crises.* New York: Norton, 1968.

Funk & Wagnalls New Standard Dictionary of the English Language. New York: Funk and Wagnalls, 1963.

King, P. M. "William Perry's Theory of Intellectual and Ethical Development." In L. Knefelkamp, C. Widick, and C. A. Parker, (Eds.), *New Directions for Student Services: Applying New Developmental Findings,* no. 4. San Francisco: Jossey-Bass, 1978.

Knefelkamp, L. L., and Slepitza, R. L. "A Cognitive-Development Model of Career Development—an Adaptation of the Perry Scheme." *The Counseling Psychologist,* 1976, *6,* 53–58.

Levinson, D. J., and others. *The Seasons of a Man's Life.* New York: Knopf, 1978.

Pascarella, E. T. and Terenzini, P. T. "Informal Interaction with Faculty and Freshman Ratings of Academic and Non-Academic Experience of College." *Journal of Educational Research,* 1976, *70,* 35–41.

Perry, W. G., Jr. *Forms of Intellectual and Ethical Development in the College Years.* New York: Holt, Rinehart and Winston, 1970.

Perry, W. G., Jr. "Cognitive and Ethical Growth: The Making of Meaning." In A. W. Chickering and Associates, *The Modern American College.* San Francisco: Jossey-Bass, 1981.

Rest, J. R. "Developmental Psychology as a Guide to Value Education: A Review of 'Kohlbergian' Programs." *Review of Educational Research,* 1973, *44* (2), 241–259.

Russell Thomas is associate professor, department of counseling and personnel services, and a member of the staff of the Center for the Study of Higher Education, the College of Education, Memphis State University, Memphis, Tennessee.

Patricia H. Murrell is professor, department of counseling and personnel services, and a member of the staff of the Center for the Study of Higher Education, The College of Education, Memphis State University, Memphis, Tennessee.

Arthur W. Chickering is distinguished professor of higher education, department of educational and psychological foundations, and director of the Center for the Study of Higher Education, the College of Education, Memphis State University, Memphis, Tennessee.

The successful implementation of a mentoring-transcript project
requires careful planning, implementation, and evaluation in
addition to institutional support and commitment.

Implementation of a Mentoring-Transcript Project

Vernon Williams
Dolores Simpson-Kirkland

As seems true in the case of every successful innovation, a mentoring transcript project needs at least one enthusiastic, committed proponent to get it
started. Provided that the idea appeals sufficiently to at least a small group of
colleagues or that the initiator has a sufficiently compelling personality,
reputation, or campus standing, the project will achieve at least pilot status.
Before even a pilot project can be launched, however, two preliminary steps
are necessary: A planning group must be organized, and project goals and
the general plan of the project must be specified. These steps are particularly
critical in implementing a mentoring-transcript project. (For an overview of
the entire process, see Figure 1.) Getting started and deciding on the nature
of the project will be discussed next, followed by consideration of specific
approaches to gaining campus support and implementing the project.

Getting Started

Planning Group. A planning group is needed to institute a project as
large in scope as arises from the mentoring-transcript concept. This group
may be initiated by someone within any unit on campus. Although the
group may at first be composed of interested persons primarily from the

R. Brown and D. DeCoster (Eds.). *New Directions for Student Services: Mentoring-Transcript Systems*
for Promoting Student Growth, no. 19. San Francisco: Jossey-Bass, September 1982.

Figure 1. Program Development Checklist

We offer this checklist as a way to try to assure yourself that you have touched the most important bases. It incorporates suggestions from Chapters One through Three as well as this chapter.

_____ 1. Organized a planning group
_____ 2. Decided on a mentoring-transcript program
_____ 3. Obtained student affairs administrative support
_____ 4. Touched bases with relevant academic administrators
_____ 5. Outlined publicity program
_____ 6. Made specific appeals to faculty and staff
_____ 7. Examined ways to obtain project recognition (grants, articles, conferences, presentations, and testimonials)
_____ 8. Developed mentor recruitment plans
_____ 9. Developed student recruitment plans
_____ 10. Designed specific mentoring-transcript plans (e.g. mentoring process, transcript formats)
_____ 11. Designed evaluation plan (see Chapter Six)
_____ 12. Developed management system
_____ 13. Established a plan for institutionalization through special project status or through integration with the organizational structure

same campus unit (campus activities, the counseling center, or the dean's office), it is desirable that group members be drawn from a variety of campus areas if it is to have the best chance to organize and implement the multitude of tasks essential to the success of the project. In addition to the matters included in the overview given here, there are dozens of meetings to schedule, letters to write, contacts to make, training sessions to design, evaluations to plan, and documents to develop. All of these tasks demand careful attention by the planning group. Four to seven people representing a variety of campus agencies or units should provide the breadth of experience, knowledge, and campus coverage to ensure interest among others on campus as well as make it possible to distribute responsibilities and tasks reasonably.

Once the project begins operation, the planning group becomes the coordinating group. A management system can be established to identify critical tasks, assign due dates and responsibilities for those tasks, and designate an overall coordinator to see that all responsibilities are met. The magnitude of the organizational challenge may seem overwhelming at first, but the rewards to be gained make the challenge worth the effort.

Deciding on Project. One of the first tasks of the planning group will be to decide on the nature of the mentoring-transcript project they wish to implement on their campus. The first three chapters of this sourcebook describe variations a mentoring-transcript project might take. The specific form for your campus depends upon the type of institution, the philosophical orientation of the institution and individual members of the planning group, the expected levels of budget support, and levels of interest of key administrators and staff members. We recommend that before you seek support for the project you arrive at a general picture of what type of project you wish to implement. After having all the planning group read over the varied forms described in Chapters One through Three, it should be possible to arrive at a consensus of one or two forms your planning group believes would work best for your campus. Once you have decided what type of project you want to implement, you can explore ways to obtain support from others on campus.

Developing Campus Support

A mentoring-transcript project has the potential to attract broad interest from campus groups including faculty, administrators, students, and parents. Their first reaction will most likely be positive, but you must realize that some may see the project as impinging upon their duties and rights. Some faculty and administrators may see it as taking over advising responsibilities, while others may see it as undermining the academic goals of the institution or as an additional administrative hassle. The planning group needs to consider carefully how it will approach administrators, faculty, staff, and students for support. It must have some idea of what the program will be like when it is implemented and what kind of support it needs. Support could range from budgetary support for special staff, released time for current staff, or sufficient moral support to initiate a project and give it a reasonably high priority within current job responsibilities.

Administrative Support. Administrators must be aware of the program if there is to be any chance of winning their support. It is helpful to arrange individual visits with at least the campus chief executive and his or her chief academic and student affairs administrators.

Key deans may also merit individual visits. Intermediate level administrators can profitably be invited to a group briefing or sent printed program descriptions. In any case, care must be given to the approach. It is all too easy to ignore a mimeographed note or a standard invitation. Everyone knows instances in which a dean played a larger role in the demise of an innovative program than did the chief campus administrator.

Once permission for an interview has been obtained from each of the top level administrators, a decision must be made concerning the request to be presented. Our recommendation is to start with the highest level of support one might hope to receive, and if that is refused, descend in stepwise fashion until assent is gained. For example, if one professional position is the most that can be hoped for, the request should begin there. From there it might go to a secretarial position, supplies, a public statement, a letter of support, and a persuasion attempt with a key colleague. The more that is known in advance regarding the administrator's position, of course, the more this descending-order bargaining procedure can be short-circuited. A tight budget year may mean it is pointless to ask for dollar support, and at times a risk may be known to exist in asking for such specific support as a public statement.

In addition to these forms of support, an excellent way to tie an administrator to a mentoring-transcript project is to ask him or her to serve as a mentor. Little can substitute for the direct satisfaction of assisting students to learn and grow as they do in the mentoring relationship. Many administrators express regret about the loss of opportunity for direct inter-action with students, and, therefore, most will accept readily an opportunity to serve as mentors. Once the process has begun, the inherent gratification will usually maintain the administrator's interest in the project.

Faculty and Staff Support. As important as top level administrative support may be, a project can fail without the support of faculty and staff professionals. Direct face-to-face solicitation of support is most effective. On a small campus or in a self-contained unit on a larger campus (for example, student affairs, an undergraduate college, or a residence education program), it is possible to make presentations to individual units (departments, halls). The most desirable approach consists of a project description, including aims, processes, benefits, and evaluation plans. Individuals may be approached sometime later for a more concrete commitment. Even if the only support needed or sought may be the goodwill of the group, identifying one or more advocates within a particular unit can be helpful.

General awareness can be achieved on a large campus by means of campus-wide or unit newsletters, news releases, and letters addressed to all faculty or staff. Some cautions must be observed. The clarity of this communication needs careful attention. The communication must be designed so that it does not appear to overstep the faculty's definition of their own turf.

Additional means of persuasion can encourage staff support. Perhaps the most meaningful persuasion involves recognition for the project, which can come in many forms. External recognition may be the most effective. A federal or foundation grant can gain considerable attention, particularly if local reporters are persuaded to do feature articles on the project. The campus newspaper is likely to be interested in any project promising benefits for students, and the university information office usually is eager to display the institution's ability to attract outside funds. Area radio networks, television interview shows, and the like are usually accessible to the college or university information office. The audience of interest for project purposes, of course, does not consist of off-campus persons, but of institutional staff members hearing or reading that the project has gained some recognition from nationally prominent professional colleagues.

Similar approaches to publicizing the project may be taken with other forms of recognition, listed here in descending order of desirability. A national publication may be next in order following a grant. In fact, a worthwhile strategy for a project planning group would be to agree at the beginning that each will try to publish a professional article on some aspect of the project. Perhaps of equal value is a conference or workshop organized around the project or a related theme. If neither publication nor conference is possible, a visit from a nationally-known figure is of some news value. Failing a visit, an endorsement from someone of national repute would provide some recognition. The reader undoubtedly can identify other events which might substitute for those listed here or fill in gaps left in the present list.

A different, but largely parallel, list can be created from events centering on the local campus. A grant from the campus teaching support group, for example, can be publicized in the same way as an external grant. The faculty development center is usually happy to facilitate such publicity. Similarly, publication in a campus or statewide organ, organization of a local or statewide conference, or observation with endorsement by well-known campus figures can provide recognition for the project.

Student Support. Student participation needs to be solicited early in the planning process. Using word-of-mouth, placing an article in the newspaper and actively seeking interested students should be sufficient to identify a group large enough to provide input and planning assistance. This initial group of participants then can assist in early recruitment of additional students. It is politically wise to seek early participation by at least a few well-known students who may be influential in early recruitment.

In summary, seeking support can be a time-consuming venture by itself. In considering the approaches described you need to think carefully about what level of support is needed to get a mentoring project started. Our experience with similar innovations is that starting a pilot program with minimal fanfare is most always a reasonable and readily accomplished objective. Getting external funding from the state or federal government or full financial backing with new funds from the campus president are worthy objectives, but if you wait for success at that level even a pilot version of the project will probably not be initiated. Do not hesitate to begin with whatever limited resources you have available.

Recruiting Participants and Implementing the Project

As you move toward implementing the mentoring-transcript project you will have to consider ways to recruit participants, train mentors, install the mentoring process, and develop transcripts.

Students. With the groundwork laid, the planning group should have an initial edge in gaining mentees. In addition, support and assistance may be solicited from student organizations. Leaders in several organizations may be briefed on the project and asked to solicit their memberships, or planning group members may choose key organizations to approach directly at regular meetings. Probably both approaches can be used effectively in combination.

On-campus students can be solicited through their living units. Just a few forceful advocates are often sufficient to do an excellent job of recruiting in residence halls, while at least one spokesperson per house is desirable with fraternity and sorority living units.

Staff who work closely with particular student groups can also be extremely helpful. This generalization applies especially in the multicultural area. General college advisers can be most valuable in devising approaches to undecided students. The admissions staff can contribute uniquely in identifying incoming students who need the special help and attention a mentoring project can afford. The coordinators need to decide which students they wish to target. Since including all students is impossible, a decision must be made to emphasize appeals to students who represent multicultural backgrounds, high academic risks, cultural impoverishment, social isolation, or some combination of traits such as these. It is possible, of course, to focus on a cross-section of the student body, but the important point is that project coordinators will be in a much better position if they have made an explicit choice as to whom they wish to include in the project.

As faculty begin to participate, they can be called upon to recruit students through the advising process and by permitting solicitation in classes.

Faculty and Staff. As mentioned in an earlier section, a face-to-face presentation is an excellent basis for soliciting faculty and staff participation. Since academe is organized around departments or divisions, they are the most logical, and accessible, units through which to approach professional colleagues. Thus, one strategy is to make a direct presentation to as many department units as is feasible.

Most desirably, the initial presentation will be informational, followed later by a direct solicitation. A sign-up form may be sent a week after the initial approach. Depending upon the desired intensity, a telephone call may follow the form. In a small institution, the entire faculty or the entire professional staff may be solicited. On a large campus, realism probably dictates that some efforts receive a special focus. Clearly many bases are possible for selection, but one important variable is an indication of positive inclination on the part of the department. A variety of ways to seek out positive reaction is possible: surveys, informal visits, consultation with teaching improvement staff or other key faculty, or even inquiry among acquaintances. Any hint of support from the dean's office should be sufficient reason to pursue commitment from a college.

On a large campus, a broad-gauge mailing can be used profitably to solicit faculty and staff participants once the project is established. At Nebraska we have found that a project description in the faculty newsletter yields at least a dozen respondents. If funds can be found for a letter addressed to all professional staff, a higher response can be expected than to a general note in the institutional house organ.

In the more hierarchial student affairs structure, a statement from the chief executive officer that he or she expects participation can result in a higher rate of enrollment than could be elicited from faculty by the chief academic officer. In fact, with that sort of support from the top, a relatively high proportion—probably more than half of the staff—can be expected to participate. Even so, word-of-mouth is the best source of staff recruitment. As the reputation of a successful project spreads, more and more staff members will seek participation.

Training Mentors

As a minimum, mentors need an orientation to the goals, activities, and planned outcomes of the mentoring-transcript project. We have found their needs beyond this to vary considerably from mentor to mentor. Mentors from student affairs offices usually know about goal setting, have had extensive experience working with individual students, and have a good sense of campus resources available to students. Faculty members, particularly on large campuses, may not be as knowledgeable about campus resources and referral agencies. Generally, faculty members who volunteer for the project have a strong interest in and commitment to students and reasonably good interpersonal skills. We have found that keeping mentors informed of the campus resources available to them and to students is quite helpful. Periodic meetings of small groups of mentors with a member of the planning group or an experienced mentor is an effective means for mentors to share concerns and different mentoring strategies. The provocative discussion of Thomas, Murrill, and Chickering in Chapter Four and our own experience suggest that the training needs of mentors require more thought and research. In the interim, providing mentors with opportunities to share concerns with other mentors or meet with more experienced mentors remains an effective training device.

Implementing the Mentoring Process

After students have agreed to participate in the project, the first step is to obtain information about their interests, skills, and knowledge levels. This information provides the basis from which the relationship between students, faculty, and staff can grow.

In having the students assess their own knowledge and skills, it is important to ascertain the level of comfort with which the students are operating and whether there are certain areas that could be discussed in greater detail. Such findings provide the basis on which the mentoring relationship can develop.

It is also helpful to gather information from members of the faculty and staff who have volunteered to be mentors. While self-assessment is not required of the faculty and staff because the focus of a mentoring project is on the student, it is important to give students information about mentors so that mentors and students can be matched appropriately.

It is advisable to allow students, faculty, and staff to review all applications, with mentor and student preference requests being honored when possible. It is also important to maintain flexibility within the mentoring relationship. Members of the project planning group should check with mentors and students periodically to see how the relationship is progressing. Requests for changes should be implemented as quickly as possible.

It is essential that all individuals who choose to become involved in a mentoring project be familiar with the goals, objectives, and format of the project. Orientation sessions for mentors and students can prove to be very beneficial in clarifying the purposes of the project.

The mentoring relationship is similar to a friendship in some respects, for many thoughts and concerns are mutually shared as the relationship develops. At the same time, it is important to keep in mind that a mentoring relationship is not a counseling relationship. Referrals should be made to the appropriate helping agencies if the need should arise. Even if the mentor is competent to do so, turning a mentoring relationship into a counseling relationship distorts the mentoring potential. The mentor can preserve that potential by continuing to work with the student in the mentoring relationship while the student is working simultaneously with a counselor.

Once the orientation sessions and matching of students and mentors have been accomplished, the initial meeting between the student and mentor can be arranged. The first session should be spent in general conversation and getting to know each other. This is also a good occasion to set up regular meeting times.

The amount of time committed to mentoring project activities will vary according to the interests and needs of the student, as well as the availability of the student and mentor. The average amount of time that students and mentors are involved in the project is one hour per week. We believe that a firm commitment from mentors and students is necessary for such a project to succeed and, thus, an expectation that individuals will participate for a minimum of one entire academic year is desirable.

Self-assessment. After the initial contact between mentor and student has taken place, arrangements should be made to review the student's self-assessment. It is this self-assessment which provides the basis for mentoring activities. Ample time should be set aside for discussion of the assessment results. It would not be unusual for the student and mentor to spend two or more sessions exploring the developmental areas that are outlined in the assessment. While it is important for the mentor to pay particular attention to the areas that the student has designated for further discussions and activities, it is also important that the student make the decision regarding which issues are to be addressed during the mentoring project. (See Appendix A, Student Development Self-Assessment Inventory.)

Goal-setting. The setting of goals by the student and mentor is the next step in the process. We have found it to be extremely useful for the student and mentor to work together to list the goal as well as the steps necessary to achieve the goal. A goal-setting sheet is a convenient means to document all of the goal-setting activities that occur during the project. Nothing is more satisfying than the successful completion of a task and the goal-setting sheet provides the means for the student to see the results of his or her efforts. (See Appendix C, Goal Planning Worksheet.)

The goal-setting process is repeated as goals are met or as personal interests and goals change during the course of the project.

The Contact Log. A useful tool for documenting activities that occur during the mentoring project is a log kept by the mentor. A log can contain the following information: the student's name, the mentor's name, the date of each session, the length of each session, and a brief summary of each session.

A record of the number of session should be kept also. All of this information can be included on a one-page form that is attached to the student's folder. For documentation purposes the self-assessment form, goal-setting sheets, and other relevant materials should be kept by the mentor. (See Appendix D, Contact Log.)

Developmental Transcript. The mentoring experience has many benefits. The interaction between student and mentor provides an opportunity for personal development and the establishment of a close relationship that might have not occurred otherwise. We feel that this experience is an integral part of a well-rounded postsecondary education. We also believe that documentation of the activities of the project should be summarized in a form that may be used as part of a resume or portfolio. The developmental transcript allows prospective employers, graduate school administrators, and others to review the co-curricular activities of students who have participated in a mentoring project. Because the transcript has been discussed in previous chapters, we will not elaborate on its forms and uses here.

Institutionalization

To move the trial stage to a stable state capable of sustaining the continuing life of a project, it is necessary to fit the specialized project structure into the standard bureaucratic structure of modern American higher education. Several options appear possible here.

First, it is conceivable that the planning group can simply continue to operate as a coordinating task force with little or no modification for as long as members are willing and the environment is benign. The disadvantage of this solution is that the originators have difficulty maintaining commitment on a continuing basis. Furthermore, this arrangement encourages thinking of the project as separate and experimental. Such labels prevent a project from affecting the campus at large.

A second option involves attempting to integrate each element of the program into an existing pigeonhole. The specific placement of each element depends, of course, on the nature of the institution. In some institutions the entire project could be subsumed under the dean of students or the student activities office. In other instances, it might make more sense to place different functions in different offices. Based on our experience, the essential functions which need to be carried on under some aegis are: (1) publicity and recruitment for mentors and students, (2) orientation to the project for new participants, (3) matching mentors and students, (4) some minimal monitoring function, (5) evaluation and feedback, and (6) transcript management.

Although we know of no project that has been in operation long enough yet to permit a confident judgment, we believe that if these six functions are provided, a mentoring-transcript project will survive.

A third solution to the continuation problem represents partial integration into the bureaucracy. In this form the project continues to be run by a small, committed group, but several functions are integrated into some existing part of the institution. Developmental transcripts may be deposited in the registrar's office, for example, in the dean of students' office, in the placement office, or in another convenient location, depending upon the main thrust of the project. Contact with students can be done by the student activities office. Publicity may be done out of the office of the dean of students. The originating group maintains overall control and coordination, making general decisions about the operation. Although we do not claim it is free from defects, we prefer this approach to the other two. The initiators are more likely than anyone else to maintain commitment to the project. Thus, they can perform the residual functions that cannot be transferred to others. By the same token, the coordinators do not have to keep commitment at the level required for total responsibility. Those parts integrated into existing student affairs offices will provide the stimulus to encourage involvement by staff in those areas. In these ways this arrangement avoids the disadvantages of the two earlier options.

If a mentoring-transcript project is to continue to exist, decisions must be made about each of the issues raised in the preceding paragraphs. Of course those decisions must be right for the particular campus on which the project occurs. We urge most strongly that the initiators suit their strategy to the organization in which they find themselves. Undoubtedly, consultation from someone not directly involved in that institution would be helpful. In any event, we offer our support and encouragement to anyone attempting to start such a venture.

Evaluation of the mentoring project is valuable for several reasons. Feedback from mentors and students allows the project director and planning group members to discover the range of the experiences in which students and their mentors have been involved. An evaluation tool also provides an opportunity for mentors and students to comment and make recommendations concerning the various aspects of the project. The members of the coordinating group are then able to review and revise those aspects of the project that warrant attention. This aspect of the mentoring-transcript project is described in more detail in Chapter Six.

Institutional commitment and support are important variables which contribute to the successful establishment of a student development mentoring-transcript project. It is also important for the project director to solicit participants in a coordinating group. The group should assume the responsibility for organizing, planning, and implementing the various aspects of the project. The third element that is crucial to the establishment of a successful mentoring project is student, faculty, and staff involvement. Careful planning, recruitment, and orientation are key ingredients for the successful establishment of a student development mentoring-transcript project.

Vernon Williams is director of the Counseling Center and professor of educational psychology and social foundations at the University of Nebraska-Lincoln.

Dolores A. Simpson-Kirkland is assistant to the dean of students and a doctoral candidate in the Department of Educational Psychology and Social Foundations, University of Nebraska-Lincoln.

*Effective evaluation of a mentoring-transcript program should
provide information to assist those who are responsible for making
decisions about the program.*

Evaluation of
Mentoring-Transcript Programs

Jane E. Baack

When planning a mentoring-transcript system, it is easy to overlook the
necessity of providing an evaluation process. For many people, evaluation
means a function that is thought of at the last minute, often after the
completion of a project, and is paid little attention by staff and administrators.
Evaluation must be an integral part of the planning from the beginning if
mentoring-transcript systems are to improve and planners and administrators
hope to make useful decisions.

This chapter discusses evaluation of mentoring-transcript systems
and the specific plan of evaluation of the Student Development Mentoring-
Transcript Project at the University of Nebraska-Lincoln. The chapter
includes a definition of evaluation, the role of the evaluator, the types and
purposes of evaluation, the key issues to be considered when developing the
evaluation plan, and an example of a model used at the University of
Nebraska-Lincoln in 1980 and 1981.

Evaluation

Evaluation is something we all do every day as we make judgments
about the worth of a program or activity. Evaluation can be a very formal,
planned activity or an informal, casual, and spontaneous subjective reaction

R. Brown and D. DeCoster (Eds.). *New Directions for Student Services: Mentoring-Transcript Systems
for Promoting Student Growth,* no. 19. San Francisco: Jossey-Bass, September 1982.

to an experience. Evaluative judgments have their greatest impact when they lead to decisions. Decisions to change a program, delete aspects of it, or discontinue the program altogether may be made because of an evaluation. An evaluation plan of a mentoring-transcript system should provide information to assist those who are responsible for making improvements in the program and to aid decision makers who must decide if the program is effective, should be retained or terminated.

The role of the evaluator is an important aspect of the evaluation plan. Ideally, the evaluator should be included in the beginning stages of planning for implementation of a mentoring-transcript system. In addition to the responsibility for gathering and analyzing data and compiling a final report, an evaluator should assist in the judgment and decision-making process throughout the program. Brown (1978) suggested that we view the evaluator as a change agent working with or for those who are committed to promoting program improvement. It is inappropriate to bring in an evaluator at the end of a project and expect him or her to understand all that has taken place in the process before being consulted. The evaluator must be a key member of the planning committee from the beginning to be able to provide timely information and suggestions for change. The evaluator should have a thorough knowledge of the goals and objectives of the project, and be free to monitor the process, noting problems as they occur and suggesting solutions.

Types of Evaluation

Different types of evaluation have different purposes and should be used according to the needs of a specific evaluation plan (Brown, 1980).

Formative versus Summative Evaluation. Formative evaluation is designed to assist program planners during the developing stages of implementation of a mentoring-transcript process. The evaluator is called upon to provide information to program planners on a regular basis, as he or she observes the process. The evaluator must be able to describe what is going on in the process, what actually occurs as mentors work with students. If planned events do not occur, the evaluator must report this to those reponsible for the program. Formative evaluation can often be provided by a staff member who has been a participant observer from the initial stages of planning. The reports are usually timely, frequent, and informal. Formative evaluation is especially appropriate when the mentoring-transcript program is in an initial pilot phase and during early stages of full implementation. This is a time when staff need information quickly on how well the program is working and where the trouble spots might be.

Summative evaluation, on the other hand, is more appropriate after a mentoring-transcript program has been in place for a time and decisions about continuing or expanding are being considered. Summative evaluations are more concerned with the products or outcomes of a mentoring-transcript system than the process. The reports may deal with student and faculty levels of satisfaction, and behavioral and attitudinal change. The reports often take the form of a final, wrap-up report on the project. Often these are formal, written reports which are forwarded to decision makers who must decide upon the worth of the entire project as opposed to planning staff who deal with the worth of component parts or aspects of the program. A summative evaluation report usually summarizes a project over a specific period of time and is carried out by an external evaluator whose purpose is to provide decision makers with information on which to base their decisions regarding the project.

Internal and Informal versus External and Formal Evaluation. Internal and informal evaluations are often a part of a formative plan, whereas external and formal reports are the products of a summative evaluation. It is frequently useful to have an insider participate as a formative evaluator. The staff member will have a thorough knowledge of the specifics of the mentoring-transcript project and will be able to respond to any unexpected deviations from the master plan.

Many people prefer to have a disinterested, objective evaluator conduct a summative evaluation to enhance credibility. This is particularly appropriate if the evaluation client or audience is external. A chancellor or a faculty committee, for example, will probably place more credence in an evaluation conducted by a person not directly involved in the program.

Program versus Personal Evaluation. It is important to limit an evaluation of a mentoring-transcript program to the program itself, not the staff who are planning it, or the students, faculty, and staff who are conducting the program. There is a great deal of fear about evaluation when people feel that they are being judged as to how closely to some ideal or model they performed. Faculty, for example, have expressed concern about whether they are "doing it right" or that their relationship with their student is "what you had in mind." The people involved need to be reminded that there is no "one best way" or "right" model for them to follow during the mentoring process. Various aspects of the program are being evaluated but the participants need not worry about being formally evaluated.

Key Steps When Planning an Evaluation

Robert Stake (1975) outlined a dozen steps for conducting a responsive evaluation. These steps have been shortened and adapted for use in planning a responsive approach to evaluating a mentoring-transcript project.

Identify the Purpose of the Evaluation. Is the evaluation information intended primarily for the project planners for use in monitoring the project while it is going on, to provide insights for ways to improve the project next year, or to provide information regarding the worth of the program for decisions about its continuance? Varying purposes require different kinds of evaluative information and data collection techniques.

Determine Who the Decision Makers Are and Their Information Needs. The issues, needs, and priorities of individual decision makers may be quite different. Faculty members may want to know if students are satisfied with the mentoring relationships and whether they consider it to be an improvement over a typical advising program. Planning staff may want to know more about what topics are discussed during a typical mentoring session. The vice-chancellor of student affairs or the dean for academic affairs may want to know if the results of the mentoring-transcript project justify the amount of time spent on it by staff members. The evaluation plan, including data collection and dissemination techniques, should consider the needs of all potential decision makers and audiences.

Identify the Key Issues. As indicated in Chapter Two, there are likely to be strong levels of support on each campus for projects like a mentoring-transcript program. However, there are also likely to be pockets of resistance. Identify what these issues are on your campus and where the resistance resides. Do some faculty see it as an invasion of their prerogatives? Do some student affairs staff members see it as extra work? Know what the issues are before the data collection process begins.

Determine How You Will Obtain Relevant Information. It is helpful to develop an information matrix which includes the basic issues as the starting column on the left margin followed by detailed statements on what type of information is most related to each issue, where the information can be obtained, when it will be obtained, and how it will be obtained. This helps guarantee that information will not be collected just because it might be interesting, but will be collected because it pertains directly to important issues. It also helps ensure that important information needs are not neglected.

Get Others Involved in Planning the Evaluation. Seek out staff, administrators, students, and relevant others as you plan the evaluation. Get as many people involved as possible and check with them frequently to learn if the evaluation plan meets their needs.

Keep in Touch. In evaluations designed to monitor the mentoring process and to improve the overall functioning of the mentoring-transcript project, frequent informal reports to staff and interested others are particularly important. This ensures that the information is reported when it is timely. Sometimes all it takes is a note or phone call to correct a mistake in assignment of mentors and students, for example. If this need is discovered early, it should be reported as soon as possible so changes can be made.

Change Directions and Plans when Necessary. A responsive approach to evaluation, unlike a formal experiment, should be flexible. Redirect your efforts if need be. Add a key issue or two as new concerns arise. Staff and faculty may discover that seniors have information needs unanticipated by mentors who were only familiar with the needs of freshmen. A changing economy or political climate may result in students being concerned about different topics. If several students need referral to more intensive counseling or therapy settings, this may prompt mentors to consider screening students prior to participation. If these concerns cannot be met during the on-going evaluation, they can be part of next year's evaluation.

Be Prepared to Write a Formal Report. A mentoring-transcript project requires a heavy investment of time and energy by a variety of faculty and staff. It may be a significant departure from previous programs and it may hold the potential for considerable expansion and impact on the rest of the campus. Word-of-mouth reports may suffice during the early phases of a mentoring-transcript project, but whether successful or not, and perhaps especially if successful, evaluative information should be available to key decision makers. Eventually, some form of a written report should be presented.

The Evaluation Plan at the University of Nebraska-Lincoln

During the fall semester of academic year 1978–79, a group of seven educators at the University of Nebraska-Lincoln worked with sixteen students in a first effort to implement the Student Development Mentoring-Transcript concept. The students who participated were enthusiastic in their praise of what occurred during their one-semester experience. Faculty and staff were also enthusiastic with the project and were willing to continue their relationship with their students. At the same time, members of the project planning staff expressed a need to have a complete description of the various activities and transactions which had taken place between students and mentors. In addition, they wanted to know the strengths and weaknesses of the program as perceived by the students, mentors, and themselves.

When plans were being made to expand the project, evaluation was included as part of the process. The main purpose of the evaluation was to describe and evaluate the Student Development Mentoring-Transcript Project *process* and, to a lesser extent, to describe and evaluate the project outcomes or *products.* Participants' judgments about the process were obtained and analyzed. The formative evaluation was used by the planning group to make decisions for the next phase of the project—to include more students and mentors. In addition, the evaluation was used to provide others interested in the project with a complete, written description of the project.

Selection of Evaluator. Serving as project evaluator was a student affairs staff member who had been one of the seven educators originally planning the pilot implementation of the mentoring-transcript project. In addition to serving as a member of the planning staff she also served as a mentor for two students. The evaluator accepted suggestions from the planning staff for key issues to be included in the evaluation plan. Some of the planning staff believed it would be beneficial to compare the mentees' experience with their mentors to that of a comparable group of students who experienced the traditional academic advising system. It was not possible to use a randomly selected control group, as all students who sought participation in the mentoring-transcript project were mentees. Data obtained from a reasonably comparable student group, however, made some comparisons possible. The purpose of surveying another group of students was to get a general description of their experiences with their advisers, to learn of their opinions of the advising system, and to compare these with experience of students who were in the project.

The evaluator attended weekly meetings of the planning group, all large group meetings held for mentors and students, the orientation sessions, and training sessions. The evaluation plan was adopted by the planning staff and the evaluator modified it as needed as the project developed. A graduate student assistant also coordinated many aspects of the evaluation effort.

Selection of Evaluation Model. Robert Stake's responsive approach to evaluation provided the basic framework for the evaluation plan and activities (Stake 1967, 1975). Elements of Daniel Stufflebeam's CIPP (Context, Input, Process, and Product) Model were also included (Stufflebeam, 1973). Stake's approach was judged to be particularly appropriate for the evaluation because he emphasizes providing a clear description of process and because he stresses that evaluation must constantly involve the client, in this case the planning group, while planning and implementing the evaluation design. Stake's evaluation strategy is based on what people do naturally to evaluate things: "they observe and react" (Stake, 1975). According to Stake, an educational evaluation is a responsive evaluation if it emphasizes the activities of the program more than the objectives. Stake believes that the evaluator should present the client with an accurate portrayal of the program. This provides clients with a description of the program as it really is, not as they wish it to be (Stake, 1975).

Following the steps suggested by Stake, the evaluator and planning group refined the list of data needs and agreed upon procedures and instruments to be used for gathering data. Following Stake's recommendations for data sources, there was an emphasis on questionnaires and interviews, as well as ancedotal records and descriptions. Data needs, the expected source of the data, and the method for obtaining the data were outlined. Both process and outcome concerns were included in this outline. Finally, a timetable for the evaluation plan was established. The evaluation plan outline is shown in Appendix E.

Data Sources. Questionnaires and structured interviews were the major source of data for the evaluation. All mentors ($N = 25$) and students ($N = 30$) completed and returned questionnaires to the evaluator and each was interviewed for about thirty minutes by the evaluator or her assistant. This was done at the end of the first semester's experience with the mentoring-transcript project. In addition, mentors maintained weekly logs in which they recorded the frequency and length of visits with their students, discussion topics, problems or areas of concern, and opinions they had reached regarding their students. Some information on achievements and goal or task accomplishment was in the form of self-reports from the students to the mentors. New mentors had opportunities to meet in a small group with a more experienced mentor or member of the planning group and some evaluation information was gathered from these reports.

The group of students who provided information on their experiences with the traditional advising system completed a questionnaire and the self-assessment inventory.

Key Issues Evaluated

The following section briefly describes some of the key issues which were evaluated, representing the chief concerns of the majority of decision makers.

Student Satisfaction and Change. This dimension of the evaluation sought to determine if students were satisfied with their experiences in the Student Development Mentoring-Transcript Project, what they viewed as the strengths and weaknesses of the process, and how they had changed as a result of participating in the program.

In order to determine their overall satisfaction the following topics were addressed:

1. How frequent were meetings with mentors during the semester and did they meet as often as the student felt necessary? Who was responsible for arranging meetings, how comfortable was the student in arranging to meet the mentor, and how easy was it to get together? Who was responsible for the content of the meetings?

2. What was the level of satisfaction with progress made toward personal education and increase in knowledge of available resources to meet personal objectives?

3. Would students recommend this experience to others, would they want to continue to meet with their mentor, and what was their overall evaluation of their participation in the project.?

Students who participated in the project were overwhelmingly positive about their experience. They had frequent (four to nine or more) meetings during the semester with their mentors, which usually lasted about one hour, and felt that they met as often as necessary. Students usually shared the responsibility to arrange meetings with their mentor, felt comfortable to arrange a meeting with their mentor, and most found it fairly easy to get together. They shared the responsibility for the content of their meetings with their mentor. Students were generally satisfied with the progress they made toward personal education through participation in the project, and were very satisfied with their increased knowledge of available resources to meet needs. By a large majority (78 percent), students indicated they would like to continue meeting with their mentor, would go to their mentor for advice or help regarding a personal concern (93 percent), would recommend the project to their friends (96 percent), and felt that their participation in the project was a "very good" or "good" experience (93 percent). Interviews revealed that the personal, shared relationship with a faculty or staff member was of greatest value to them. Greatest change was reported to be in ability to assess strengths and weaknesses and to set priorities and goals.

Faculty and Staff Satisfaction and Change. An almost identical set of questions regarding meetings (length, frequency, responsibility for arranging, content, and ease of arranging) revealed that mentors were also satisfied with this aspect of the project. They, too, enjoyed the shared responsibility of the mentoring relationship.

The majority (60 percent) of mentors reported that participation in the project has "somewhat" or "greatly" increased their satisfaction with their role as an educator. Many (78 percent) reported that participation in the project enabled them to work in a new way with the mentees. A significant result, revealed in interviews, was that the vast majority believed their participation in the project had caused them to deal with their other students in new and different ways. The carry-over of the mentoring concept and philosophy was greater than the planning staff had anticipated.

All mentors wanted to continue to meet with their students, 96 percent would "definitely" or "probably" recommend the project to their colleagues and felt that their participation had been a "very good" (44 percent) or "good" (52 percent) experience.

Goals for Students

Planning staff had numerous goals for students who participated in the program but they wanted to evaluate three specific goals regarding self-assessment, goal-setting skills, and creation of a personal development transcript.

Self-Assessment. Almost all students (93 percent) found the self-assessment inventory, developed for use in this project, to be "very" or "somewhat" helpful. The mentor and student used this instrument as a tool to initiate their relationship, to determine what areas of development the student wanted to focus on, to locate priority areas of concern, and to assess the student's strengths and weaknesses.

At the end of the semester, the majority (74 percent) of students were satisfied with their increased ability to assess their strengths, weaknesses, and skills.

Goal Setting. Most of the students (89 percent) indicated they found the process of setting goals as developed by them and their mentor to be "very" or "somewhat" helpful. A majority (59 percent) indicated they were satisfied with their increased ability to set and manage goals. A majority (89 percent) were satisfied with their level of goal achievement during the semester. Career-related goals were indicated most frequently as those that had been identified to work on with their mentor.

Transcript Creation. Almost none of the students actually created a personal development transcript. Many of the students really did not understand the concept or the rationale for the transcript, they did not feel the need to create one, or the mentor never introduced the idea as a potential goal for the semester.

The evaluation revealed that in this area the goal of the planning committtee was not met. Students were overwhelmingly positive about the process of the project, the mentoring relationship, but they had not produced one of the anticipated outcomes. Several stated that they might create a transcript in the future so a follow-up evaluation may reveal more about this aspect of the project.

Goals for Faculty and Staff

Interviews with faculty and staff mentors revealed that they considered the orientation and training sessions, held before participation in the project, to be the weakest part of the program. Some mentors felt the material covered in the training sessions was too basic and did not take into account the various levels of advising expertise of the different mentors. Others suggested that it would have been helpful to have had a more thorough explanation of how a "model" mentoring relationship might be expected to progress.

Most felt they had not had enough exposure to the concept of a developmental transcript. Some planning group staff who also were mentors met with small groups of mentors once or twice during the semester. This was viewed as a valuable experience by the great majority of those who attended these sessions and it was suggested by several mentors that small groups should meet more frequently to discuss how the process was developing. Comparing notes with other mentors in the company of an even more experienced mentor or planning staff member was highly valued.

Attitudes and Opinions of Key Decision Makers

Planning Staff. Planning staff members were also concerned that the training sessions had not been as satisfactory as they had planned. Another concern was how to include more lower division students, minorities, and those entering freshmen who were in the third and fourth quartile of their high school class. There was a sense that the project was not reaching these students who might also benefit from such a personal relationship with a faculty or staff member.

Administrators. The vice chancellor for student affairs and the associate dean of Teachers' College were two key decision makers because most of the mentors were staff or faculty members under their supervision.

The vice chancellor for student affairs served as a mentor to express his support for the student development mentoring-transcript concept and to work with a student on a more personal basis than was usually possible in his administrative role. He was extremely positive and enthusiastic about the experience. Earlier, he had expressed concern about the time commitments required to be a mentor. When interviewed, he felt that the time was well spent because the student with whom he worked had gained so much from the experience. He, too, felt that he had profited from the process.

The associate dean of Teachers' College was very positive in his support of the concept and the project. He suggested that Teachers' College mentors should be asked to speak at faculty meetings about their experiences and to urge others to join the project. He felt that, because of the tremendous time commitment for faculty mentors, written reports of their experiences would be put in their files in order to document institutional recognition and support of their efforts.

Descriptive Portrayal

Information gained from all of the data sources about the mentoring students has been summarized into a descriptive portrayal. Though not a factual report of an actual student's experience, this descriptive portrayal is a composite of a typical mentoring experience and, when compared to a descriptive portrayal of a typical advising experience, is very revealing.

Portrayal of a Mentoring Experience. Sue, a sophomore participant in the mentoring-transcript program, is anxious to meet with her mentor today so she arrives a little early for their usual Wednesday afternoon meeting. Carol Williams, professor of English, is waiting in her office. Carol is reviewing her notes from last week's session with Sue and makes a note to ask Sue several questions. She is ready to meet with Sue at the scheduled appointment time. Sue can hardly wait to share with Carol the information she has gained since last week's appointment. On Carol's suggestion, Sue had phoned the career planning and placement center on campus and had made an appointment with one of their staff members. This person suggested she talk with two or three people. Eventually she talked with an officer of a local bank who thought her idea of "shadowing" a bank officer for several days had merit. Carol and Sue had been thinking of ways Sue could test her tentative desire to get an MBA and become a bank officer. Carol suggested that other staff members on campus were able to help her with specific details of career planning and Sue found that to be a helpful referral. Sue was trying to make decisions about potential careers and Carol had already helped her focus her information seeking and to set some goals regarding career plans. Carol was not only a great adviser on academic and career matters, but Sue felt that she really cared about her as an individual. She considered Carol a friend and would go to her with any concern that might arise during her years in college. She felt very fortunate that her adviser/mentor was not like the one assigned to her friend, Joe.

Portrayal of an Advising Program Experience. Joe, a sophomore, usually went to see his assigned adviser only once a semester and for one reason only–his signature was required on the course list which had to be turned in at the time of preregistration. Joe had not yet declared a major and because he was in the second semester of his sophomore year he was getting anxious. He went to his adviser's office during the office hour for the week and waited in a line outside the office. Joe finally got in to see Professor Smith of the economics department at the end of the office hour. He explained his concern about his undeclared major status and wondered aloud if he would be able to make up his mind about what major to declare by his junior year. Professor Smith mentioned that business and computer science seemed to be the two "hottest" majors at the time and that there were lots of jobs for graduates of those majors. Joe mentioned that he had enjoyed most of the liberal arts classes he had taken. Professor Smith suggested that he ought to be practical. Joe was not exactly sure what that meant. He started to ask another question about how to balance the practical type of courses with the ones he enjoyed most, but was interrupted by Professor Smith who stated that his office hour was up and that Joe would have to make up his mind soon about his major because the filing deadline was approaching. Joe felt he had been hurried out of the office before he had even gotten to ask the most important questions. Professor Smith did not seem to care about him or his problems and never suggested who might be able to help him. Joe wondered why they even called it an advising system.

Recommendations for Improvement

After analyzing all the data from an evaluation study, it is helpful to review the purposes of the evaluation and to select information on the agreed-upon key issues. In addition, any final reports should reveal major strengths and weaknesses plus any serendipitous findings. As already indicated, students, mentors, and planning staff all offered some suggestions for improvements. Major changes suggested were a review of the orientation/training sessions for mentors, more small groups, more emphasis on the transcript concept with some specific examples furnished to students and mentors, one or two more large group meetings for students and mentors to share experiences with one another, and future studies to learn more about retention and satisfaction rates of students in the project.

90

Summary

A carefully planned evaluation strategy must be an integral part of any mentoring-transcript system. The Nebraska evaluation plan and results serve as a concrete example of an evaluation strategy developed to fit the specific needs of the clients and decision makers. Another mentoring-transcript system might require a different evaluation plan but the basic issues may be quite similar. While plans and ideas are adaptable to many campuses, each will have to identify the key issues and information needs relevant to the particular campus and situation. The following guidelines can serve as a checklist as you plan for and conduct an evaluation:

1. Identify the purpose of the evaluation.
2. Decide who are the decision makers.
3. Identify the key issues which each decision maker believes must be addressed by the evaluation.
4. Identify how you will obtain the data or information you need.
5. Get as many people as involved as possible and check with them frequently to learn if your plan meets their needs.
6. Develop an evaluation plan based on a conceptual model which fits the needs of the program and the people involved.
7. Make frequent, informal reports.
8. Be flexible. Redirect your efforts if necessary. Be willing to change the evaluation plan if necessary.

References

Brown, R. D. "How Evaluation Can Make a Difference." In G. R. Hanson (Ed.), *New Directions for Student Services: Evaluating Program Effectiveness,* no. 1. San Francisco: Jossey-Bass, 1978.

Brown, R. D. "Evaluating Learning Centers." In O. T. Lenning and R. L. Nayman, *New Directions for College Learning Assistance: New Roles for Learning Assistance,* no. 2. San Francisco: Jossey-Bass, 1980.

Stake, R. E., "The Countenance of Educational Evaluation." *Teachers' College Record,* 1967, *68,* 523–540.

Stake, R. E. *Evaluating the Arts in Education: A Responsive Approach.* Columbus, Ohio: Merrill, 1975.

Stufflebeam, D. L. "Educational Evaluation and Decision-Making." In B. R. Worthen and J. R. Sanders (Eds.), *Educational Evaluation: Theory and Practice.* Belmont, Calif. Wadsworth, 1973.

Formerly the assistant to the dean of students at the University of Nebraska-Lincoln, Jane E. Baack is currently a staff member of the career planning and placement center at the University of California-Berkeley and lecturer in the School of Business at San Francisco State University.

Personalizing the learning process through mentoring-transcript programs can enhance the individual growth of educators as well as students and contribute to the revitalization of postsecondary institutions.

Mentoring-Transcript Programs and the Future Needs of Higher Education

Robert D. Brown
David A. DeCoster

During one of the early evaluations of the mentoring-transcript program at the University of Nebraska-Lincoln, students were asked, "What is the difference between a mentor and your adviser or a counselor?" Many professionals find the distinctions difficult to make, seeing the possibility of a sizable overlap in roles. Students were not expected to do any better. Instead, their responses were immediate and they had no problem distinguishing roles and characteristics. As one student said,

> Oh, there are clear differences! There are no comparisons with an adviser? (Giggle) I hardly ever see my adviser. Lately, I sign my own registration forms so I don't need to see my adviser at all. I don't think my adviser even knows who I am. (Nervous laughter) I guess I think of a counselor as someone I would go to if I had a problem. I wouldn't be afraid to see a counselor, but I think it would be necessary only if something was bothering me.
>
> My mentor is somebody different. He is somebody more like a friend. I can trust him and I can talk to him about most anything.

R. Brown and D. DeCoster (Eds.). *New Directions for Student Services: Mentoring-Transcript Systems for Promoting Student Growth*, no. 19. San Francisco: Jossey-Bass, September 1982.

I can even drop by just to say, 'Hi' and I would never do that with my adviser or counselor. My mentor knows me and I suspect we will be in touch after I graduate.

Similar comments have been made by other students since the inauguration of the mentoring-transcript program.

Prognosticators, looking at the next two decades in higher education, predict increasing alienation among students, greater diversity among new student populations, more faculty and staff morale malaise, more conflict between faculty and students, and general retrenchment of programs. We believe the appropriate response to these portentous possibilities should be an openness to innovation, as called for by the Carnegie Council (1980). College administrators need to manage for excellence rather than for survival and stability (Balderston, 1974). In this closing chapter, we suggest that the mentoring-transcript concept, though not the cure-all for education's ills, can be an innovation that will: (1) personalize education, (2) be responsive to new student needs, (3) assist faculty and staff development, (4) promote understanding between students and faculty, and (5) assist the revitalization of postsecondary institutions.

Personalizing Education

People are more likely to spend time today with persons of the same age and less time with people older or younger than themselves at any time in our history (Hareven, 1978). Generations are essentially segregated and the three-generation household is an anachronism. As a result of this trend and others, traditional college-age youth are exposed to fewer older adults than their parents or teachers were. Students' models for maturity and wisdom are likely to be what television and other media portray rather than people they meet and associate with in their daily life. Toffler (1980) even suggests that friendships, as we know them today, will become difficult to establish and maintain, as people in the next two decades will work in different settings with highly individualized schedules. It may be necessary, according to Toffler, to "schedule-a-friend," much as we now dial for a prayer, our daily horoscope, or advice for the lovelorn.

Colleges are far from immune to impersonalization and, though the student of the early eighties appears placid and sanguine, there is increasing evidence that insecurity and alienation are not far below the surface (DeCoster and Mable, 1981). A mentoring-transcript program can be particularly relevant for the potentially alienated or isolated student. Students who are shy, naive, or hostile to the college can benefit from participation. The shy student who is uncomfortable in approaching a faculty or staff member for advice on academic or personal matters may respond to the accessibility of a proactive, empathetic mentor. Building a developmental transcript can add to this student's self-esteem and confidence, reducing insecurities and shyness. The naive student could find the process helpful in learning what the college offers for total personal growth and how to cope with the system. Hostile students who believe college life is a battle between the system (faculty, staff, and regulations) and themselves could learn that individuals within the system care and will listen.

A mentoring program personalizes the educational process in a way that cannot be done by even the most dynamic and sincere instructor behind a podium or the most attentive financial aid adviser behind a desk. As mentoring-transcript programs are initiated and evaluated, special efforts are needed to recruit students who are shy, naive, or hostile and to assess the impact of the mentoring-transcript program on their personal development and attitudes toward the institution.

Responsiveness to New Students

A decade ago, Pat Cross (1971) alerted us to the influx of new students of the sixties and the need for higher education to be responsive in the seventies. Most predictions for the future suggest the trend toward an ever-changing student body composition will be increasing rather than tapering off. The Carnegie Council (1980) predicts that by the year 2000, 50 percent of students will be over twenty-two, 85 percent will not live on campus, 45 percent will be part-time, and 25 percent will be minorities. Overall, nearly one half of the students by the year 2000 would not have been there if the composition of college students remained what it was in 1960. These new students will have different needs, competencies, and aspirations than the students of 1960. Postsecondary institutions will have to review programs, services, and even traditions carefully if they are to be responsive.

At least two groups of new students, minorities and the nontraditional, are likely to derive unique benefits from the mentoring process and the transcript product. Minority students make less use of advising systems and have more difficulty relating to faculty than majority students (Willie and McCord, 1972). It is unlikely they will be assigned or readily find an adviser who is similar in race or ethnicity. Generally, they are more likely to be socially isolated (Fleming, 1981) and have more trepidation about knocking on an authority figure's door. They are probably also more naive about the opportunities for personal growth within an institution. The mentoring-transcript process provides these students with built-in access to a mentor from whom they can seek guidance about the system as well as about themselves. The transcript process and resulting product serve also to encourage a goal-setting orientation to personal growth rather than a perspective that hopes for survival and sometimes little more.

Nontraditional adult students also have special needs and concerns (Tough, 1981). Their situation is analogous, if not identical, to that of minority students. They are often unacquainted and uncomfortable with registration, advising, and other bureaucratic management systems. They are uncertain of their own competencies and goals and insecure about being in classes with younger students. The peer group, a powerful force affecting traditional age students, is less likely to be a source of advice or support, especially if the older students are not able to associate with peers in age as well as status. Nontraditional students are more likely to be lost, confused, and bewildered about what is expected of them and what opportunities may be open to them. The availability of a mentor provides these students with an age peer and a model. The transcript process and product also provide them with an opportunity to assess past accomplishments and develop skills in articulating their competencies.

Faculty and Staff Development

Reduced mobility, increasing pressures because of more rigorous promotion and tenure policies, and retraining needs because of retrenchment and reallocation decisions are just a few reasons why faculty and staff concerns will demand increasing attention in the next decade or more. Thomas, Murrell, and Chickering in Chapter Four suggest that mentoring relationships with students provide faculty and staff an opportunity to fulfill generativity needs for those who wish to see their work and values carried on by the younger generation. The faculty member can work with a mentee in a different, more personal, role than instructor or adviser. Faculty member and student know there will be no grade given at the end of the term and the relationship can carry on beyond the semester. This adds a dimension to the relationship between faculty and students not otherwise readily possible at the undergraduate level.

Student affairs staff members involved in mentoring relationships see themselves as fully implementing their espoused philosophy of promoting development of the whole student and doing so as a student development educator (Brown, 1980). As mentors, their role is different than a counselor or activities adviser. They can work with the mainstream of students, not just the troubled or the highly active student. Depending upon how the mentoring-transcript program is implemented, the opportunity to work directly with students as educators and with faculty as colleagues and in consulting roles may be extensive. These relationships enhance the professional pride and status of student affairs staff members.

Understanding Between Faculty and Students

It is important to recognize the potential existence of hostility as well as a gap between generations. A generation conflict may exist that is attributable to parent, teacher, faculty, and staff attitudes as much as to student behavior. Feuer (1969) believed student rebellions were inevitable and most student rebellions through history have ended up being irrational and self-destructive. He attributed causes to student immaturity and failure to work through the oedipal conflict. A more recent viewpoint, however, suggests the generation conflict is also caused by parents and other adults. Sheleff (1981) posits what he calls the "Rustum complex" as an equally valid explanation for generational conflict. The Rustum complex, taken from a Persian tale, suggests parents have a built-in antagonism toward their children that may result in indifference, contempt, and even open attack and ultimate destruction. The source of hostility is dislike for nurturing tasks, problems accompanying social change, fear of death, and hope for immortality. Viewed within the context of postsecondary education, it is possible to hypothesize that faculty and staff have paradoxical attitudes toward students. They are expected to be nurturing and encouraging as they assist students in their learning. But students also reflect societal changes and youthful enthusiasm, resiliency, and resistance and represent threats to faculty who see themselves less involved with current issues as well as perhaps physically and psychologically burnt out. Sheleff suggests recognition of the Rustum complex may be sufficient if it leads to humility and the wisdom to appreciate the responsibility that should accompany power over the young. Ideally, it should also provoke a search for new patterns of relationships between elders and novices. The mentoring dimension of the developmental transcript system provides mentors a source of information about students and another way to learn the implications of an elder's power. Several authors (Perry, 1970, Sanford, 1980) suggest that interviewing students is one of the richest data sources about students and also one of the major ways of having an impact on students. The mentoring role puts the faculty or staff member in the position of listening and learning, which should increase their understanding of students.

Institutional Revitalization

Each institution implementing a successful mentoring-transcript program will reap several benefits. Though it is too early to provide comprehensive evaluative data, it seems reasonable to assume that students involved in mentoring programs are more likely to stay in college and complete their academic programs. Analogous data from studies of advising programs indicate successful programs result in higher retention rates (Lenning and others, 1980). Colleges that provide opportunities for students to interact with faculty on an informal basis, as well as in the classroom, also have higher retention rates (Pascarella and Terenzini, 1977). There is every reason to believe that successful mentoring-transcript programs will have the same effect. Not only will retention rates be affected but the existence of a mentoring program is likely to have value for recruitment purposes. Students who feel they need or can benefit from more personal attention are likely to be attracted to institutions that make special efforts to meet these needs. Institutions that listen to what students have to say through their mentors are also likely to be alert to other needs of students. This, in turn, should assist the institution in being responsive to students throughout the campus.

The benefits accrued by personalizing the educational process for students, faculty, and staff cannot help but have further direct and indirect benefits for the vitality of the institution. Satisfied students are like satisfied customers who will speak highly of their institution to others. Educators who experience positive feedback regarding their professional roles are likely to contribute in many ways to the institution's vitality. Lockland (1973) suggests that "mutuality," a willingness to be changed as well as to change others, is a necessary prerequisite for growth. Faculty, staff, and administrators can profit by considering how assisting the personal development of students can foster mutuality and result in institutional, as well as personal, growth.

Conclusion

Two major assumptions underlie the student development mentoring-transcript concept. First, the primary goal of education is to promote the fullest possible development of each student. Development is broadly construed to include growth in interpersonal skills, emotional maturity, esthetic interests, career choice, moral values, and health awareness and physical fitness, *as well as* intellectual competencies and knowledge. Second, the relationship between academic-intellectual and personal development is symbiotic. As Sanford (1980) says, "There is no more effective instrumentality for personality development, in young people and in adults, than the curriculum in the hands of people who know how to use it" (p. 127). Intellectual and personal development cannot be separated without some loss in the value and effectiveness of one or the other. Promoting the development of the whole student does not diminish the value of cognitive growth but rather enhances it.

It is natural in a period of limited budgets and retrenchment to question whether now is the appropriate time to encourage administrators to consider programming for development of the whole student (Strange, 1981). It is also important, however, to consider the consequences if we do not try. The continuing need over the next several decades to reallocate resources makes it even more essential for colleges and universities to examine ways to personalize education.

The mentoring-transcript program models described in this volume, though diverse, represent only a few of the possible variations. These need to be tried and validated through evaluation studies, research, and the test of time. Mentoring-transcript programs may never become as widespread as traditional advising systems and academic transcripts. Some small institutions are establishing programs on a systemwide basis while larger schools often work with a small percentage of their total student population. After three years of operation at the University of Nebraska, for example, the voluntary program serves approximately sixty students and utilizes about forty mentors. Thus, as options, such programs provide students with a means to pursue personal development intentionally and provide colleges and universities with another method to keep faculty and staff vibrant and their institutions responsive.

References

Balderston, F. E. *Managing Today's University.* San Francisco: Jossey-Bass, 1974.

Brown, R. D. "Student Development Educator." In U. Delworth and G. Hanson (Eds.), *Student Services: A Handbook for the Profession.* San Francisco: Jossey-Bass, 1980.

Carnegie Council on Policy Studies in Higher Education. *Three Thousand Futures: The Next Twenty Years for Higher Education.* San Francisco: Jossey-Bass, 1980.

Cross, K. P. *Beyond the Open Door: New Students to Higher Education.* San Francisco: Jossey-Bass, 1971.

DeCoster, D. A., and Mable, P. *New Directions in Student Services: Understanding Today's Students,* no. 16, San Francisco: Jossey-Bass, 1981.

Feuer, L. S. *The Conflict of Generations: The Character and Significance of Student Movements.* New York: Basic Books, 1969.

Fleming, J. "Special Needs of Blacks and Other Minorities." In A. Chickering (Ed.), *The Modern American College.* San Francisco: Jossey-Bass, 1981.

Hareven, T. K. "Historical Adulthood and Old Age." In E. H. Erikson (Ed.) *Adulthood.* New York: W. W. Norton, 1978.

Lenning, O. T., Beal, P. E., and Sauer, K. *Retention and Attrition: Evidence for Action and Research.* Boulder: National Center for Higher Education Management Systems, 1980.

Lockland, G. T. *Grow or Die.* New York: Random House, 1973.

Pascarella, E. T., and Terenzini, P. T. "Patterns of Student-Faculty Informal Interaction Beyond the Classroom and Voluntary Freshmen Attrition." *Journal of Higher Education,* 1977, *48,* 540–552.

Perry, W. G., Jr. *Forms of Intellectual and Ethical Development in the College Years: A Scheme.* New York: Holt, Rinehart and Winston, 1970.

Sanford, N. *Learning After College.* Orinda, CA: Montaigne, 1980.

Sheleff, L. *Generations Apart.* New York: McGraw-Hill, 1981.

Strange, C. "Organizational Barriers to Student Development." *NASPA Journal,* 1981, *19,* 12–20.

Toffler, A. *The Third Wave.* New York: William Morrow, 1980.

Tough, A. "Interests of Adult Learners." In A. Chickering (Ed.), *The Modern American College.* San Francisco: Jossey-Bass, 1981.

Willie, C. V., and McCord, A. S. *Black Students at White Colleges.* New York: Praeger, 1972.

Robert D. Brown is professor of education, Department of Educational Psychology and Social Foundations, University of Nebraska-Lincoln.

David A. DeCoster is dean of students and associate professor, Department of Educational Psychology and Social Foundations, University of Nebraska-Lincoln.

Appendixes

APPENDIX A

College Student Development Self-Assessment Inventory
Developmental Mentoring-Transcript Project
University of Nebraska, Lincoln

Introduction

This inventory provides an awareness of the many dimensions of personal growth that might be addressed during the college years. It offers you the opportunity to rate yourself on two aspects related to these dimensions: (1) your present level of competency for each area, and (2) how satisfied you feel about your abilities. Thus, the inventory is intended to get you thinking about yourself and to help you create an overall profile of your personal development. Continued growth will occur through the campus environment. Your ability to set goals and identify activities that fulfull your objectives are important factors that can enhance this educational process.

Directions

The inventory lists 56 different dimensions clustered in six major areas of personal development. You are asked to answer three questions related to each item.

1. What is your proficiency or knowledge level? Circle the appropriate number after each item according to the following legend:
   1 = Very Low
   2 = Low
   3 = Uncertain
   4 = High
   5 = Very High
2. How satisfied are you with your ability in this area? Circle the appropriate number in the second column after each item according to the following legend:
   1 = Very Low
   2 = Low
   3 = Uncertain
   4 = High
   5 = Very High
3. Would you like to talk about this topic to either get a better idea of your skills or find out how you might improve? Circle either "yes" or "no" in the third column after each item.

Sample Item:

Being a leader of a group   5 4 ③ 2 1   5 4 3 ② 1   (Yes) No

101

The response to the sample item indicates that the individual is uncertain or confused about his or her skills on this dimension, is somewhat dissatisfied with this proficiency level, and would like to discuss this topic in the future.

College Student Development Self-Assessment Inventory

Name: _____ Sex: _____ Age: _____

Major: _____ Year: FR SO JR SR

Ethnic Background: _____ Hispanic   _____ Black
                   _____ Asian American   _____ White
                   _____ Native American   _____ Foreign National

I. *Personal Identity and Life Style*	Proficiency Level High Low	Satisfaction Level High Low	Further Discussion
1. General Lifestyle Goals	5 4 3 2 1	5 4 3 2 1	Yes No
2. Self-Knowledge	5 4 3 2 1	5 4 3 2 1	Yes No
3. Moral and Personal Values	5 4 3 2 1	5 4 3 2 1	Yes No
4. Problem Solving Skills	5 4 3 2 1	5 4 3 2 1	Yes No
5. Self-Assessment Skills	5 4 3 2 1	5 4 3 2 1	Yes No
6. Time-Management	5 4 3 2 1	5 4 3 2 1	Yes No
7. Sexuality	5 4 3 2 1	5 4 3 2 1	Yes No
8. Spiritual & Religious Values	5 4 3 2 1	5 4 3 2 1	Yes No
9. Career Planning & Choice	5 4 3 2 1	5 4 3 2 1	Yes No
10. Ability to set and achieve goals	5 4 3 2 1	5 4 3 2 1	Yes No
11. Self-Sufficiency Skills	5 4 3 2 1	5 4 3 2 1	Yes No
12. Other _____	5 4 3 2 1	5 4 3 2 1	Yes No

II. *Multi-Cultural Awareness*

Understanding of other:

13. Religions	5 4 3 2 1	5 4 3 2 1	Yes No
14. Cultures and Races	5 4 3 2 1	5 4 3 2 1	Yes No
15. Countries	5 4 3 2 1	5 4 3 2 1	Yes No
16. Members of my own culture of the opposite sex	5 4 3 2 1	5 4 3 2 1	Yes No
17. Other _____	5 4 3 2 1	5 4 3 2 1	Yes No

	Proficiency Level High ... Low	Satisfaction Level High ... Low	Further Discussion
III. *Interpersonal Skills and Relationships*			
18. Being an effective member of a group	5 4 3 2 1	5 4 3 2 1	Yes No
19. Being a leader of a group	5 4 3 2 1	5 4 3 2 1	Yes No
20. Relationships with same sex friends	5 4 3 2 1	5 4 3 2 1	Yes No
21. Relationships with opposite sex friends	5 4 3 2 1	5 4 3 2 1	Yes No
22. Relationships with parents	5 4 3 2 1	5 4 3 2 1	Yes No
23. Public speaking skills	5 4 3 2 1	5 4 3 2 1	Yes No
24. Developing intimate relationships	5 4 3 2 1	5 4 3 2 1	Yes No
25. Teaching, Advising, and Helping Others	5 4 3 2 1	5 4 3 2 1	Yes No
26. Other _____	5 4 3 2 1	5 4 3 2 1	Yes No
IV. *Academic Skills and Intellectual Competencies*			
27. Study techniques	5 4 3 2 1	5 4 3 2 1	Yes No
28. Reading speed & comprehension	5 4 3 2 1	5 4 3 2 1	Yes No
29. Note-taking	5 4 3 2 1	5 4 3 2 1	Yes No
30. Writing skills	5 4 3 2 1	5 4 3 2 1	Yes No
31. Working with numbers	5 4 3 2 1	5 4 3 2 1	Yes No
32. Listening skills	5 4 3 2 1	5 4 3 2 1	Yes No
33. Humanities	5 4 3 2 1	5 4 3 2 1	Yes No
34. Natural Sciences	5 4 3 2 1	5 4 3 2 1	Yes No
35. Social Sciences	5 4 3 2 1	5 4 3 2 1	Yes No
36. Specific Vocational Skills	5 4 3 2 1	5 4 3 2 1	Yes No
37. Other _____	5 4 3 2 1	5 4 3 2 1	Yes No
V. *Aesthetic Awareness* Knowledge and appreciation of:			
38. Music	5 4 3 2 1	5 4 3 2 1	Yes No
39. Art	5 4 3 2 1	5 4 3 2 1	Yes No
40. Drama	5 4 3 2 1	5 4 3 2 1	Yes No
41. Literature	5 4 3 2 1	5 4 3 2 1	Yes No
42. Dance	5 4 3 2 1	5 4 3 2 1	Yes No
43. Other _____	5 4 3 2 1	5 4 3 2 1	Yes No

	Proficiency Level		Satisfaction Level		Further Discussion	
	High	Low	High	Low		

Performance:

44. Music	5 4 3 2 1	5 4 3 2 1	Yes No
45. Art	5 4 3 2 1	5 4 3 2 1	Yes No
46. Drama	5 4 3 2 1	5 4 3 2 1	Yes No
47. Literature	5 4 3 2 1	5 4 3 2 1	Yes No
48. Dance	5 4 3 2 1	5 4 3 2 1	Yes No
49. Other _____	5 4 3 2 1	5 4 3 2 1	Yes No

VI. *Health, Physical Fitness, and Recreation*

50. Health habits	5 4 3 2 1	5 4 3 2 1	Yes No
51. Nutritional knowledge	5 4 3 2 1	5 4 3 2 1	Yes No
52. General fitness	5 4 3 2 1	5 4 3 2 1	Yes No
53. Hobbies	5 4 3 2 1	5 4 3 2 1	Yes No
54. Recreational skills	5 4 3 2 1	5 4 3 2 1	Yes No
55. Use of leisure time	5 4 3 2 1	5 4 3 2 1	Yes No
56. Other _____	5 4 3 2 1	5 4 3 2 1	Yes No

VII. Is there anything else that you would like to relate about yourself and your personal development? (Use reverse side for additional space)

APPENDIX B

Mentoring-Transcript Clearinghouse Contact Persons for Mentoring and Transcript Projects

Institution	Contact Person
Alverno College (Wisconsin)	Austin Doherty
American College Testing Program (Iowa)	Michael W. Ham
Andrews University (Michigan)	Gary L. Dickson
Azusa Pacific University (California)	Raymond P. Rood
Canisius College (New York)	Thomas E. Miller
College of Saint Teresa (Minnesota)	Margaret Pirkl, OSF
Educational Testing Service (New Jersey)	Lee L. Schroeder
Michigan State University	Anthony E. Stapleton
Notre Dame College of Ohio	Sister Mary Marla, S.N.D. and Sister Mary Donald Ann, S.N.D.
Pine Manor College (Massachusetts)	Judith L. Sanford
Salem State College (Massachusetts)	Robert G. Caruso
University of Iowa	Linda M. Carucci
University of Maryland	Janice L. Kirkpatrick
University of Minnesota Technical College	Herb Atwood
University of North Dakota	William A. Bryan and Greg T. Mann
University of Wisconsin-Madison	Paul Ginsburg and Jack Kellesvig
University of Wisconsin-Stevens Point	Florence Guido-DiBrito
Westmont College (California)	Keith McLellan

Note: This information based on self-reported materials submitted to Mentoring-Transcript Clearinghouse as of January 1982.

APPENDIX C

Goal Planning Worksheet

1. List a goal. _____

   Note: Is it specific?
   Is it realistic—that is, consistent with my personal characteristics, abilities and opportunities?

2. Describe how you will know when you meet this goal.

   _____

   _____

   _____

3. Brainstorm all the possible steps that could be involved in your reaching that goal. Number the steps in the order that you will need to perform them. Use the extra space to list sub-steps if needed. For example, if one step is to interview a professional in your field, a sub-step may be compiling a list of people you might contact about an interview with them.

   __ A. _____

   _____

   __ B. _____

   _____

   __ C. _____

   _____

   __ D. _____

   _____

   __ E. _____

   _____

   __ F. _____

   _____

4. Questions to consider and discuss: What is the timeline to complete each step? How will you know when you have completed each step? Describe how you will reinforce your commitment to meet each step in the process.

APPENDIX D

Student Development Mentoring-Transcript Project
Log of Mentor-Student Sessions

Student

Mentor

Session #	Date	Length of Session	Summary of Session

APPENDIX E

Outline of Evaluation Plan

Project Process

Data Need	*Source*	*Method of Collection*
1. Orientation to concept of mentoring and developmental transcript	1. Mentors and Students	1. Questionnaire
2. Recruitment and selection of mentors and students	2. Mentors, students and planning group	2. Questionnaire
3. Mentor training sessions	3. Mentors and planning group	3. Questionnaire/ Interview
4. Small group sessions for mentors	4. Mentors and planning group leaders of small groups	4. Questionnaire/ Interview and logs of small groups (kept by leader)
5. Large group meetings for students, mentors and planning group	5. Students, mentors and planning group	5. Questionnaire
6. Use of Self-Assessment Instrument	6. Students and mentors	6. Interview
7. Goal-Setting process	7. Students and mentors	7. Interview
8. Recording of development (transcript)	8. Students and mentors	8. Interview
9. Closure at end of semester	9. Students and mentors	9. Questionnaire

Project Products or Outcomes

1. Satisfaction with and attitude about project	1. Students and mentors	1. Questionnaire and interview

111

2. Perceptions of students' change in transcript areas	2. Students and mentors	2. Self report and mentor reports Self-assessment inventory
3. Perceptions of ability to utilize resources	3. Students and mentors	3. Self-report and mentor reports
4. Perceptions of self-assessment skills	4. Students and mentors	4. Interview and mentors reports
5. Commitment to the project	5. Students and mentors	5. Questionnaire and Interview
6. Attitudes about students' development goals	6. Mentors	6. Questionnaire
7. Anticipated and unanticipated benefits of participation	7. Mentors	7. Interview and Questionnaire
8. Strengths/weaknesses of small group sessions for mentors	8. Mentors and planning group	8. Questionnaires
9. Perceptions of skills and mentoring	9. Mentors	9. Questionnaire and Interview
10. Attitude about need for student development transcript	10. Mentors and students	10. Questionnaire and Interview
11. Evaluation information during process	11. Planning group	11. Interview
12. Corrections for future management project	12. Planning group	12. Interview and Questionnaire

Index

implementation of, 73–75; process of, 15; relationships in, 10–14; and sexual harassment, 62; skills in, 11–13

Mentoring-transcript systems: alternative models of, 33–48; assumptions in, 96; and audience diversity, 60–61; evaluation of, 79–90; and faculty and staff development, 94; and faculty-student understanding, 94–95; and feasibility issues, 60–64; and goal setting, 75; and higher education needs, 91–97; implementation of, 67–77; and institutional revitalization, 95–96; institutionalization of, 75–77; and new students, 93–94; planning group for, 67–68, 75–76; project for, nature of, 68–69; recruiting participants for, 71–73; starting, 67–69; support for, developing, 69–71; theoretical bases for, 49–60

Mentors: and assessment, 61; defined, 49; evaluation of, 63, 77; functions of, 10; mentee fit with, 52–53, 62–63; as models, 53–57; potential, 14, 61–62; training of, 63, 73

Michigan State University: contact person at, 105, Lifeline program at, 35; outcomes ranking at, 9

Miller, T. E., 105

Miller, T. K., 48

Minnesota Technical College, University of: contact person at, 105; Student Development Transcript at, 38

Modeling: effects of, 54; and motoric reproduction, 55–56; theory of, 53–57

Murrell, P. H., 2, 49–65, 73, 94

N

Narratives, transcript as, 25–26

Nebraska-Lincoln, University of: evaluation at, 79, 83–85; faculty recruitment at, 72; Mentoring-Transcript Clearinghouse at, 33–48, 105; outcomes ranking at, 8–9; potential mentors at, 14; Student Development Mentoring-Transcript Project at, 9–10, 97, 101–104

Nelson, R. B., 30, 48

North, R. A., 30, 48

North Dakota, University of: Co-Curricular Transcript at, 45–47; contact person at, 105

Northwest Area Foundation, 43

Notre Dame College: contact person at, 105; Model for Student Development at, 35; portfolio at, 38

P

Parker, C. A., 8, 17

Pascarella, E. T., 6, 11, 17, 54, 57, 64, 95, 97

Perry, W. G., Jr., 50–53, 62, 64, 95, 97

Pflum, G., 30

Pine Manor College: Comprehensive Advising System for Students at, 39; contact person at, 105

Pinkney, J. W., 23, 31

Pirkl, M., 105

Portfolios, transcripts as, 26

Preston, M., 30

Prince, J. S., 35, 48

Progoff, I., 23, 31

R

Record keeping, growth and, 22–23

Rest, J. R., 50, 51, 64

Roche, G. R., 10–11, 17

Rood, R. P., 2, 40–42, 105

Rose, M. P., 17

Rustum complex, 95

S

Saint Teresa, College of: contact person at, 105; Developmental Objective/Transcript Program at, 43–45

Salem State College: contact person at, 105; Student Activities and Development Record Card System at, 37

Sanford, J. L., 105

Sanford, N., 95, 96, 97

Sanstead, M., 16, 30

Sauer, K., 97

Schroeder, L. L., 105

Self-assessment: and development, 28; by students, 73–75, 86

Shapiro, E. C., 11, 17

Sheleff, L., 95, 97

Simpson-Kirkland, D. A., 2, 67–77